Hindsight

The Unraveling Effects of Addiction

Denise Williams

Fulton Books, Inc.
Meadville, PA

Published by Fulton Books 2020

ISBN 978-1-64654-576-6 (paperback)
ISBN 978-1-64654-577-3 (digital)

Printed in the United States of America

It's been sixteen months now since I buried my son, Ryan, due to a heroin overdose. As I move on in life, I still find myself looking back and asking how things went so wrong. Like so many other parents who have walked in my shoes, we all say the same thing after burying our beloved child, "I wish I knew than what I know now" and "Why didn't I speak up before?" I'm sure I will take these regrets to my grave.

I have three children—twin sons, Ryan and Matthew, and a daughter, Katie, who is two years younger than the boys. I have been married to the same man, Tim, since 1981. It's not a happy marriage, by any means, but we are still here.

I would consider our lives, until 2007, pretty good. I truly loved life. The only real tragedy was that our first son, EJ, was stillborn in 1983. Back then, a stillbirth child was whisked away from the mother almost immediately. I never got to say hello before I had to say goodbye. I still carry that sadness with me today.

I gave birth to Ryan and Matt in 1985 and then to Katie in 1987. We lived in the suburbs, in small town Pasadena, Maryland. We weren't rich by any means, but we had a great life and were very happy. The kids thrived. They were all very active in school, sports, and social events. All five of us had many friends in the community. We also spent a lot of time with Tim's and my family, who we were extremely close to. In my opinion, we had it all, and I couldn't have been happier.

As the kids grew older, they seemed to remain happy-go-lucky. They were easy to raise and never got in to any real trouble. They also seemed to find their own niche. Ryan was the athlete, Matt played music, and Katie found creativity in experimenting with makeup and hairstyling. Their personalities defined who they were. Ryan was the very outspoken, funny guy. Matt was the quiet, polite, people pleaser, and Katie was a momma's girl with attitude. Ryan and Katie were a lot like Tim, and Matt was a lot like me. Good or bad, filtered or not, I loved that they were each their own person.

I just wonder how everything I thought was so perfect could go so wrong?

As they approached their late teens, my only advice to them was, "You don't have to be the best, but you do the best you can and always live life with no regrets."

It turned out *regrets* is the one word that haunts everyone in the family so deeply.

During their final years in high school, Ryan pretty much stayed focused on his running, cross-country, and track and field. Katie spent most of her time with cheerleading and student government. Matt, our quiet and "perfect" son, became quite the rebel. He started smoking pot and drinking. I found out years later, there were also other drugs he was doing. He wasn't getting in trouble at school or with the law, but he was turning into a party boy. Tim's opinion and my opinion on how to handle Matt were polar opposite. Tim thought it was just a phase he was going through, and his punishment should have been minimal—grounded for a weekend but okay to have friends over. I thought we needed to be much stricter—grounded for two weeks, no car, no friends over. Tim ended up getting his way because I don't like controversy. It was much easier for me to give in without a fight even though my head was saying, "This is wrong." Still, I chose to remain silent. I regret it.

Over the next few years, I'm ashamed to say, there were several underage drinking parties at my house. The first one was Ryan and Matt's senior prom night. I overheard some of their friends talking about going to an after-prom party at another friend's house in Bowie, Maryland (about thirty minutes away from our house). The child's father was going to be out of town. No parents would be supervising the party. I was very upset and confronted Ryan and Matt about it. They didn't deny anything but simply told me I couldn't stop them from going. According to them, they were eighteen years old and could do whatever they wanted.

Tim thought we should just let them have a small party at our house after prom instead. This way, they wouldn't drink and drive, and we could supervise them. We would not supply any alcohol, but we'd provide a safe environment for them to have fun. The voice in my head was saying, "Oh my god, are you insane? We could go to jail if the kids bring alcohol!" Instead, I told them I'd think about it. After about two weeks of pressure from Tim, Ryan, and Matt, I gave in. I agreed to host an underage drinking party at my house.

I set a few rules: (1) beer only, no hard liquor; (2) everyone was to remain at our house all night—I was going to collect all keys; (3) everyone had to eat and drink water if they were drinking beer. Thank God, no one got drunk, and everyone remained safe.

As parents who agreed to host an underage drinking party at our house, we could have lost everything that night. Looking back now, I did lose a lot that night. Ryan and Matt viewed me as a pushover. All my kids had to do was join forces with their father, and I would cave to their demands. They were too young to have a father who was their buddy and a mother who was a pushover. Over the next couple of years, there continued to be parties at my house. I knew about some, but most happened when Tim and I were away at the beach.

As time passed, Matt continued to drink heavily and use drugs. His drugs of choice were marijuana and cocaine. It was getting more and more out of hand. He came in all hours of the night (or morning) completely wasted and disruptive to everyone. We all agreed that it would be best if Matt moved out.

Even though Ryan remained focused on his schoolwork and running, he was dabbling more and more in pot and drinking. This was going on mostly during college breaks and summer months. Katie soon started following in her brothers' footsteps. I was seeing all this happen before me and kept asking why. All three of my kids hated when their father drank, which was all too often. Now all three of them were doing the one thing they disliked the most about their father. I saw them spiraling out of control and did nothing. Another regret.

The next few years of our lives continued to spiral. Ryan got arrested for selling a small amount of pot. Matt used every last bit of his savings to buy cocaine. Katie continued to worry me but more for her choices in boyfriends than her partying.

Matt

I thought my life came to an end on January 17, 2007, when at 4:15 a.m., I received a phone call from the University of Maryland Medical Center at Shock Trauma. Matt had been in a car accident, and we needed to come quickly. They were preparing him for emergency surgery. He broke, chipped, dislocated, or crushed almost every bone in his left arm and hand. He broke a leg, cracked, and bruised his ribs and had minor lacerations all over his body. He also suffered a concussion. Matt's toxin screen came back, showing he had high amounts of cocaine, pot, and alcohol in his system. We all knew Matt had a substance abuse problem, but none of us did anything to try to control it.

Matt underwent seven operations and spent three to four days per week in physical therapy over the next two and a half years. His injuries prevented him from ever playing his beloved guitar ever again. Matt became very depressed.

What happened over the next nine years made the previous four seem like child's play. It was obvious that Matt, with his extensive injuries, surgeries, and therapy, would need pain medication. He was prescribed OxyContin and Percocet. Matt had never taken pills recreationally before. He actually had a hard time adjusting to them. During his first week home, it was not uncommon for him to vomit after taking his medications. He said he hated them but was in so much pain that he needed them. He initially took the prescribed amount of pills, but after about two months, he craved more and more. Matt started subsidizing them with illegally purchased OxyContin and Percocet.

In August of that same year, Matt was hospitalized with sei-zures. His neurologist said that more than likely, he had suffered a seizure the morning of the car accident. I found out that Matt had been having blackouts and seizures for quite some time but hadn't told me. The doctor said his seizures were triggered by smoking, drinking, and drug use.

By the one year anniversary of the accident, Matt had a $100-per-day pill habit over what was being prescribed by his doctor and therapist. Matt started using heroin because it was cheaper and easier to get. No one in the family knew. He kept it a secret.

Ryan

As Ryan's college years were coming to an end, he fell in love with a young lady. He also started using cocaine, Percocet, and drinking more and more. When the girl became pregnant, Ryan wanted to do the right thing and get married and buy a house. He started saving everything he made for a down payment. Because Ryan was abusing drugs and alcohol, he started selling on the side to afford his habit. He ended up finding a small home, something not too expensive, but it cost more than what they could afford. Ryan convinced his father to lend him a sizeable amount of money so they would qualify for a loan. Tim agreed. I spoke up and told him he should look for something cheaper, but I lost the battle. I wish I would have made my voice heard.

When the baby was born, Ryan was a great hands-on father, but he continued to party excessively. Immediately, after moving in to his new home, he wanted everything in the place to be updated and improved. He applied and got approved to any credit card he could get his hands on. His fiancée lost her job, and their debt increased.

His "dabbling" in drugs had reached a full-blown addiction. He was using drugs to hide from the realities in his life. He was drowning in debt and having serious relationship problems.

Matt

It was apparent to everyone that Matt was an opioid addict. Money, jewelry, electronics, and tools were all coming up missing from the house and from my husband's business. We were finding needles and heroin bags; capsules and crack pipes; along with other household items, such as cotton balls, Q-tips, spoons, vinegar, cutup straws, foil, and Chore Boy steel wool in Matt's room. These are all items an addict would use for drug paraphernalia.

Katie called him out on several occasions and even attempted to do a drug intervention. I backed her up but was so damn clueless. I wasn't much help. Ryan and Tim wanted nothing to do with an intervention. Tim did not believe that Matt was an addict. Ryan was barely talking to Matt because he was shooting heroin. Ryan thought Matt had crossed the line when he became an IV user. I always thought it was more because he had seen himself following in Matt's footsteps. Ryan may not have crossed over that line, but he most certainly had one foot on the line. Matt was a mirror image of what Ryan was becoming.

Tim and Katie's relationship really became strained because of the suggested intervention. They never had that great of a relationship. They were so much alike and were always fighting and butting heads. But now the relationship was damaged.

Matt was discharged from his doctor and therapist in the spring of 2009. I called the therapist and let her know that Matt was a full-blown heroin addict. At first, she was shocked and horrified. Then she got very defensive and said that she was sorry, but I needed to understand that without opiate pain medication, she could not do her job. The pain Matt would have to endure would be torture without pain medication. Wow! That was not what I expected to hear. My interpretation of what she said was that my son became an addict so she could have a job.

We were able to convince Matt (with the help of Katie's friends) and Tim that he needed professional help. It was going to be at a local outpatient health department clinic. I went with Matt to his intake interview. The first part of the intake was private between Matt and the interviewer. I joined the two after a short period. She told me that she and Matt had both agreed that a Suboxone program would probably be the best treatment. I had no idea what Suboxone was. She explained that it is a drug used in the treatment of opioid dependence. She said that Matt could start as soon as he was seen by the doctor who was on vacation at the time. He was expected back in a week. She then instructed Matt to tell me the other thing they discussed in private. Matt said to qualify for treatment, he would have to have drugs in his system when he started. You could have knocked me over with a feather! In other words, I would have to permit my son to use illegal drugs for another week. Not only that, but I would also have to be the one to buy them since Matt had no money.

Matt did get treatment, but it wasn't a week later. The doctor was on vacation for two additional weeks. Then when he returned, he had to see all his regular patients before seeing anyone new. Matt was not seen for almost two months. And yes, I kept Matt high the entire time he waited to start.

I should have asked more questions. Knowing what I know now, Matt would have only gotten the minimal amount of drugs to prevent withdrawal while waiting. Instead, he got the full amount that his body was used to. Allowing Matt to have the high amount of opiates and me being the one paying for them caused huge conflicts between Ryan, Tim, and I. I don't regret the conflict, but I most certainly regret not asking more questions. Matt only lasted about two months before being discharged from the program for dirty urine.

Ryan

Ryan's drug problems kept escalating. I would stop by his house unannounced only to find shady things going on that left a really bad taste in my mouth. It wasn't just what Ryan was doing either. There were rumors going around that drugs were being used and sold while my grandson played in the same room. There were all-night parties, and people were constantly coming and going from their house. I arranged to have my grandson go to my daughter's house while I tried to have a one-on-one intervention with Ryan. It did not go well.

Ryan was very defensive and called the police on me for kidnapping. Surprisingly, the police were on my side. They knew I didn't kidnap my grandson, but I still had to tell Ryan where he was. The police tried to get me to bring child endangerment charges against Ryan and his fiancée. Ryan's house was known to the police as a "house of interest." His neighbors had been calling in complaints for quite some time because of all the constant comings and goings and suspected drug activity.

If I agreed to bring charges against Ryan and his fiancée, the police would have had the right to search the property. If anything at all was found incriminating, they would have both been arrested and forced into treatment, and my grandson would have been placed in my custody.

I regret not bringing charges against them. I had an opportunity to force Ryan into treatment and didn't take it, knowing my grandson was in harm's way.

Matt

Matt's heroin use continued after being kicked out of the health department clinic. More and more money and items of value continued to come up missing. Tim was constantly buying back the pawned items that we knew were being stolen. I begged Matt to enroll in patient treatment. He refused to go, and Tim didn't want to pay the initial co-pay. Our house was in constant turmoil. Tim was drinking more and more and was coming home less and less.

I felt like Katie and I were left all alone to deal with the growing drug and alcohol problems. We didn't know who to talk to or where to turn. Katie finally asked her friend for help. Her friends suggested a treatment center called the Hope House. She made a call for us, and Matt had a bed waiting for him in two days. I put on my big girl pants and told Tim to pull the co-pay from our bank account, which he did. I told Matt that if he didn't go, then he could no longer live in our house. It appeared everyone was on board.

The next day, Matt told me he had a lunch date with his on-again, off-again girlfriend. She picked him up, and they never came back. She took him to her parents' house in another county about forty-five minutes away and they turned off their phones. I was able to call the girl's mother one time before she turned off her phone too. I cried while pleading with her to bring Matt back so he could get into rehab. Her response was that she didn't think Matt nor her daughter had a drug problem. I went to the rehab center the next day, hoping that Matt had reconsidered. He hadn't.

I still was not giving up on Matt. My brother suggested that I petition the court for what's called an "emergency petition" to force

Matt into rehab. Technically, the petitions are for loved ones of someone who suffers from mental health issues to force them into treatment because they may hurt themselves or others. Matt's age (now twenty-four years old) kept the judge from granting me the petition. He was an adult, and at the time, addiction was not considered a mental health issue. I cried and cried, so disappointed.

I wasn't sure where Matt was or if he was even still alive. It had been almost a week since he left. While sitting in my car crying, I got a phone call from the Montgomery County Court House in Rockville, Maryland, asking me if I planned on attending Matt's bail hearing. He had been arrested the night before for possession. I briefed her on what had transpired in the past week. She was going to try to delay Matt's hearing until I got there. Matt was going to be released on his own recognizance. While waiting for his paperwork to be completed, I called the rehab center, and they had a bed available in two days.

The forty-five-minute car ride home was nothing short of a ride from hell. Matt was going through withdrawal. It was a side of him I had never seen. He was ugly, angry, and out of control. The entire ride home, he was kicking and banging the windows. He called me every name in the book and said I should have just let him die in jail. He told me I had no right to interfere with his life. There were moments when I thought Matt was going to jump out of my car. It was by far the longest ride of my life, and I was sure we weren't going to make it home alive.

Katie was able to get Matt some Percocet to take until we took him to rehab. The next day, we went back to Rockville to meet with Matt's court liaison. She made it very clear that he had two choices—jail or rehab. Matt chose rehab.

That night before bed, Matt came to my room. I had never seen him so vulnerable. He and I were both crying. He told me how sorry he was for all the heartache he had caused. He told me he fled because he was in such constant pain that he couldn't imagine his life drug-free. Rehab scared the hell out of him. I slept well that night. I truly thought my problems with Matt were in the past.

I got a phone call from Matt's counselor three days into his treatment. She said we needed to talk immediately about Matt's mental health issues. Katie went with me to meet with the counselor. Matt greeted us at the door. He was smiling, happy, and looked amazing. I was emotional over his transformation. It was his (and Ryan's) twenty-fifth birthday. Matt said to us, "Happy birthday to me. It's the first time since I was fourteen years old that I've been sober on my birthday." That was very hard for me to hear. Where was I on all those birthdays that I didn't even know my teenage son was high? I had no idea that Matt had been using at such a young age.

I found things out about Matt at the meeting that I was completely unaware of: Matt, being the people pleaser all his life, had suppressed his true feelings. Some of it was trivial but had festered so long deep inside that it was now something major to him. Matt cried most of the time while releasing all his bottled-up issues.

He had issues with everyone in our family. One of his issues with me was that I never let him pick the theme of his and Ryan's birthday parties. He thought I should have known that this bothered him because he always said that he wished he had his own birthday and didn't have to share it. He told me that I'm his mother, and I should have known what that meant. I had no idea that's what he meant, and I felt so badly that this bothered him for all those years.

One of the most significant issues with his father was that Tim rarely attended Matt's sports games or concerts because no alcohol was allowed. He felt like his father didn't even know his name until he was old enough to sit on a barstool next to him.

After Matt was sent back to his classes, Katie and I spoke a few more minutes with his counselor. She said Matt would always have drug issues until mental health issues were addressed. She gave me a list of psychologists and psychiatrists in the area. She was going to get Matt extra time in the center until I was able to find him help. There were twenty or so names on the list. For days, I called and recalled every one. Some had an answering machine taking calls, and I never got a callback. Most were not accepting any new patients, and the rest did not accept Matt's insurance.

Matt's health insurance would only pay for a fourteen-day stay in rehab. The counselor got him an extra seven days while I tried to find a doctor. At the end of the twenty-one days, the counselor suggested that I pay out of pocket for additional days until I could find a doctor. It would be $65 per day—$65×7= $455 per week. About $910 for two weeks. This on top of the $1,500 co-pay I had already laid out. Like most average people, I could not afford this. I felt really bad, and I knew I was letting Matt down. He was discharged with no doctor. He desperately needed us, and we let him down.

Katie

Katie got married to a great guy in July of 2010. They had a beautiful beach-themed wedding and reception. Five months later, Katie gave birth to a beautiful baby boy. I believe my grandsons were the only good thing in my life that kept me going.

Matt

About two months after getting out of rehab, Matt was showing signs of relapse. Tools, copper, money, and other things were once again coming up missing. After confronting Matt, he talked about taking his own life. He could not see any other permanent way out of a life of drugs.

I called back one of the doctors from the list from the rehab who did not accept Matt's insurance. He agreed to meet Matt at the hospital. He got Matt into a two-week outpatient psychiatric program, where he was treated with antidepressants.

We decided to have Matt continue seeing the doctor at his private practice. The first available appointment was in a month and a half. He would see both a psychiatrist and a therapist. We would be paying $250 out of pocket per visit. He saw both doctors on his initial visit, but he would be alternating between the two for all visits after that. They wanted him to be seen every other week.

Just before Matt's next visit, I got a phone call from the doctor's office. They had to cancel his appointment because both doctors had left the practice. I couldn't believe it. After a couple of pleading calls to the practice, they reluctantly gave us the new phone number of one of the doctors—the one whom he saw at the outpatient program. He wasn't due to open his practice for another three months. We made Matt an appointment and hoped nothing would happen while waiting.

Ryan

As Ryan's drug use continued to increase, he became paranoid and extremely angry. There were rumors going around that his fiancée was involved with other men. Ryan was miserable. He believed he had worms and other parasites throughout his body and that they were trying to eat his insides. He picked at his skin until there were holes. He was having frequent outbreaks of MRSA and staff infection. Once when I took him to the hospital for a severe MRSA outbreak, the doctor treated the infection and then told him to get help for his obvious drug abuse because getting off drugs would prevent further outbreaks.

We urged Ryan to get treatment for his drug abuse, but he didn't think he had a problem. Rehab wouldn't fix the only problems he thought he had: financial and relationship.

That Christmas was horrible for my grandson. His parents could only afford one gift for him even though they always had money for drugs. My family stepped up and gave the child the Christmas he deserved. It really disappointed me that they chose drugs over presents for their toddler.

Matt

M att did see the psychiatrist when his office opened. The cost
was $125 for the first thirty-minute visit and $85 for each visit
after. He restarted Matt back on antidepressants and Suboxone. His
road to recovery was very short-lived. It caused increased tension at
home. Matt started staying at Ryan's house. His on-again, off-again
girlfriend started staying there too.

Ryan

Ryan and Matt and their partners were all living together. This was the worst-case scenario: four people with drug addiction living in the same house.

Ryan's fiancée was the first to admit that it was a mistake and left. She also broke up with Ryan. He took it very hard. He became extremely depressed and was cutting himself. He cut her name into his arm. Ryan came to me crying one day. He curled up on the sofa, put his head on my lap, and cried like a baby for hours. He finally admitted that he had a drug problem and was in a ton of debt. He told me how deeply his ex-fiancée had hurt him. He said he knew she had cheated on him. I wanted to call 911 to get him treatment that night. Ryan refused. He said he knew he would have to claim to be suicidal to get immediate help. He was not suicidal. He just wanted to be loved—he wanted to live. He agreed to let me take him to GBMC Greater Baltimore Medical Center the next morning for a psychiatric and drug evaluation in the hopes of them getting him into Sheppard Pratt for a dual treatment.

The next morning, Ryan was ready to go. They kept him under observation for a few hours before discharging him. They asked him several times if he was suicidal. His answer was always the same, "No, I am very depressed, I have a drug problem, and I just want to be happy." At discharge, they gave him a list of doctors whom he could go to for help. It was a lot of the same names that we had gotten for Matt at Hope House. It was a total letdown. That night, Ryan shot heroin for the first time.

The next few years went from bad to worse. Now that Ryan was also using heroin, the boys were feeding off each other's addictions. They both had several attempts at in- and out-patient treatment but never at the same time. They each also spent a few short weekends in jail. Nothing seemed to work getting and keeping them clean. Katie and I continued to try to stay one step ahead of them. As it turned out, however, they were always one step ahead of us. Matt attempted suicide two more times. One of the times, he was hospitalized for a short period.

More money, jewelry, electronics, and tools went missing. I went to a few of the pawnshops in the area. I didn't go to buy everything back. I went to vent my frustration as to how these shops were enabling addicts. I accused them of being addicts' best friends. The only thing I accomplished was to get myself banned from two of the shops. My addict sons were welcome back any time.

One time, my car was traded for a weekend of free drugs. The car was returned late Sunday afternoon. There were several receipts from fast-food places, gas stations, and convenient stores down the I-95 corridor to Norfolk, Virginia. I was told this was how the dealers allegedly brought drugs back to the area to sell.

We found three bullet holes in one of the family vehicles. Supposedly, the bullets were a warning to pay the $10 debit for the drugs they were fronted the week before.

Ryan

We had to take Ryan's custody time with his son away from him. We thought Ryan was exposing his son too much more than a three-and-a-half-year-old should be. The court granted us joint legal guardianship of Ryan's son. We shared custody with his mother. We only allowed Ryan to see his son when he was sober. It was a sad day for all of us.

Ryan's house went into foreclosure. Now I had two adult heroin addicts living in my home.

Matt

Matt was required to do a weekend in jail for a repeat offense of driving with a suspended license. Prior to his weekend in jail, Matt checked himself into a hospital for detox and mental health treatment. His hospital caseworker arranged for him to enter a forty-five-day rehab immediately after he completed his weekend in jail. The caseworker asked me to call his probation officer to make him aware that Matt was going to rehab (four hours away from the area) and would not be reporting in for his next appointment. If he agreed not to violate Matt, then he would be free to go to rehab. The probation officer wished Matt well and promised not to violate him.

On Sunday night, I went to pick Matt up from jail. He was further detained at the correction facility, and no one knew why. The only information they could share with me was that a last-minute bench warrant was issued for Matt. The warrant had no explanation. I was told to attend his bail hearing in the morning to find out why it was issued and to get things straightened out.

The next morning, the judge was also not explaining the warrant. He denied Matt's release and kept his bail at an extremely high amount. He apologized for not knowing the reason for the warrant but said he had the utmost respect for the judge who issued it. We could not afford to bail Matt out, so he was going to remain in jail.

The correction facility had no doctor on staff, and because Matt had mental health issues and suffered from epilepsy, he was to be placed in solitary confinement until a doctor could treat him. He stayed in solitary confinement for a little over a week. Matt spent a total of thirty-four days in jail until his court date. Most of that time, we did not know why he was in jail. Matt found out from his public defender that the charge was a violation of his probation. His probation officer had apparently changed his mind and violated Matt.

The judge at Matt's hearing found out then that his probation officer had not told the entire truth about Matt when he requested the warrant. He never disclosed to her that Matt was going to rehab. He also lied about Matt violating probation. When the warrant was issued, Matt technically had not violated probation yet. His probation date came during his second week in jail. Matt's charges were immediately dismissed. The probation officer got into a lot of trouble for what he did. He called the house the next day to apologize to Matt for his poor behavior, for which he had no plausible explanation.

Matt's grandmother died while he was wrongfully incarcerated, and the rehab center no longer accepted Matt since he had been drug-free for more than thirty-four days.

Ryan

There was a warrant out for Ryan's arrest for failure to appear on a traffic offense. Ryan decided to turn himself in rather than wait for the sheriff's office to pick him up. He did not want his son to see him taken away in handcuffs. Ryan was in the bathroom showering when his son knocked on the bathroom door, calling for his father. I could not hear water running and got a bad feeling when I realized Ryan was not answering. I immediately started banging on the door and calling for him too. The door was locked. I screamed for my husband and Matt to help. They broke the lock and forced the door open. Ryan had overdosed. He was unresponsive, and there was foam coming from his mouth. There was a needle and heroin baggies on the counter. We were able to revive him. I didn't let anyone call 911. I regret that.

It took several days for the heroin to leave Ryan's system. Meanwhile, he had one of the most horrifying outbreaks of MRSA. The entire side of his face swelled up and broke out. His eye swelled shut, and he had a boil-like abrasion on the center of his cheek. His face was completely deformed, and he was almost unrecognizable. He needed hospital treatment.

Katie, Matt, Tim

During these heartbreaking and frustrating years, Katie and I fought with everything in us to save Ryan and Matt. On more than one occasion, Katie followed her brothers into the area where the drug dealers lived. She would beg the boys not to make the buy. I blocked one phone number after another on Ryan and Matt's phones. I eventually just took them off my account.

When drugs were delivered directly to our house, I would use my cell phone to take picture of the car, license plate, and person(s) in the vehicle. One time, drugs were delivered after midnight in a green cab car. The dealer in the cab looked like he was ten years old. I stood my ground and made it very clear that I would call the cops if a deal went down. The standoff took about an hour and a half. That night, I won. No drugs were purchased. The next day, I called the cab company to complain. I was told there was nothing they could do since I only knew the dealer's street name and not the given name used to book the cab. I couldn't believe it! They had the time and location where the cab was. It became clear to me that cabs were used for drug deals often, and the person I was speaking with didn't want to ruin a good thing.

I wrote to Dr. Phil twice asking for help, and Matt wrote him once. We never heard back.

Matt did finally ask for treatment. We both thought Sheppard Pratt Mental Health hospital would be the best place for him. I thought back to how we tried to get Ryan help there but was denied access. I called the hospital directly and asked how one could get treatment there without being admitted by a doctor. The woman I spoke with suggested Matt go to our local hospital for an evaluation and let them know we wanted him to be referred to Sheppard Pratt. The nurse stressed how important it was that were insistent that he go to that mental health hospital, specifically.

I decided to go with Matt. I figured two persistent people were better than one. I stayed for a while and expressed my choice for a treatment facility before leaving. Matt called me later to give me the good news that he would be going to Sheppard Pratt as soon as a bed was available within the next day or two.

I got a call the next night that Matt was being transferred but was going to University of Maryland Medical Center Psychiatric ward in Baltimore City. Neither one of us was familiar with this program. We were disappointed that he wasn't going where we wanted him to but decided something was better than nothing.

Katie went with me to visit Matt the next morning. He met us at the reception desk and wanted to leave. I learned quickly that this was the wrong treatment facility for him. It did not treat depression or addiction. It only treated more severe mental health disorders like multiple personality disorder and schizophrenia.

I asked to speak with someone in charge. One of Matt's assigned therapists spoke to me. She apologized for the mix-up. She affirmed that Matt did not belong there since they did not treat his illness. But she said that Matt could not leave because they did not discharge patients on the weekend. It was Sunday. She promised she'd relocate Matt to the correct facility on Monday. He was to be transferred to a dual treatment facility not far from the hospital called the Tuerk House. The program there was to be thirty to forty-five days long. I was finally relieved.

On Monday, I helped Matt pack his things and headed to the Tuerk House, only to be told that they do intakes Wednesdays before 9:00 a.m., something the hospital didn't mention. We turned around and went home for two days. On Wednesday, when we went back, we were told that they only treat Baltimore City residents. We lived in Anne Arundel County. We were forced to leave, and I felt hopeless.

I was depressed and alone. I was aware of the stigma of addiction. I chose to remain silent rather than talk about what was happening in my own house. I had cut ties with all my friends and most of my family. As angry as I was at Ryan and Matt, I didn't want anyone judging them.

I attended a few support groups, but nothing felt right. I wanted answers, and I wanted to understand addiction. I didn't want to study the twelve steps or listen to prayer. I was praying a lot on my own, and in my opinion, if everyone lived their lives according to the twelve steps, this world would be a much better place. I wanted to know why my sons had taken on a different personality, why they were doing things that were out of character for them, and why they chose drugs over friends and family.

I found a ten-week family class at the Hope House Treatment Center, and it was perfect! The three and a half hours every Monday night for ten weeks was the best thing I did for myself since this nightmare began. I learned how little I knew about addiction. The class was broken down into three parts. First, we had a group meal and an open discussion about the challenges we faced that week. Then we had our support discussion with the counselors. We spent the remainder of the night in a classroom-like setting where we learned about addiction and mental illness and how both were destroying our loved ones' bodies and minds. Finally, I found something that I could relate to and that was helpful to my struggle and well-being.

On February 7, 2014, Tim suffered a stroke. Over the next four months, he was either in a rehabilitation center, the hospital, or had in-home care coming to our house. In April of 2014, he suffered another more severe stroke—a brain bleed. The doctors said that he was permanently disabled and would probably never work again. This resulted in him being terminated from his traveling sales job. He also lost his health insurance while still in the hospital.

My focus turned from Ryan and Matt to Tim. My number one priority was getting him health insurance. I also had to take over the family finances—something I knew nothing about nor had I done in our thirty-three years of marriage. Our finances were a mess—beyond repair. Our house was about to go into foreclosure, and every bill was months past due. To this day, I don't know where our money went and why Tim stopped paying the bills. We had suffered some hardship a few years prior when his poorly operated business went under, but we had both been working again and making decent money. He had me believing that we were doing okay. He never gave me an answer as to why we weren't.

The icing on the cake came when I found out that Tim had a woman on the side. Our marriage had been over for years, but this was a slap in the face, and it hurt my ego deeply. I stayed in the marriage, not because we were in love with each other (because we weren't) but because we couldn't afford to get a divorce.

I agreed with the bank to let our house go on the market as a short sale to avoid foreclosure. Eventually, I caught up on most of our bills. Tim was declared permanently disabled and now receives disability from Social Security.

Ryan and Matt

During the months when I focused on my and Tim's finances, Ryan and Matt got more and more out of control. There were many days when I felt like I no longer had the energy to help them. Ryan and Matt were stealing from Katie, her husband, me, and my parents. We had to bring charges against them. Katie and I went to the police station together. We told the detective that we wanted them to get help. We preferred six to eighteen months of treatment, but we understood if they had to do jail time. We did *not* want another probation before judgment.

When the charging documents came to the house, I was shocked and sickened. They each had sixty-four theft charges, and Matt was also being charged with breaking and entering, as well as burglary in the fourth degree for entering Katie's house without permission. This is not what we wanted. Most of value amounts of the items were overly exaggerated and 95 percent of the tools they had allegedly stolen belonged to Ryan. Ryan faced eighteen months in jail for stealing and pawning his own tools. Matt faced ten years—a felony conviction.

Nothing was even mentioned about a treatment plan that Katie and I discussed with the detective. I desperately wanted to undo what I had done. Why had it come to this? They both just needed long-term dual treatment, but instead, they were headed to jail. By the time Matt would have gotten out, he would have lost two decades of his life to the consequences of addiction. I regret bringing the charges against Ryan and Matt, but I also resent the lack of accessible and long-term treatment for mental health and addiction.

Even though I felt awful beyond words about the charges brought against my sons, I was still angry with them. They were both facing jail time, and yet they were still using. They both needed some sort of treatment before court. I decided to kick them out of the house, hoping with nowhere else to go, they'd choose rehab. I had a difficult time bringing myself to do it but didn't know what else to do. My biggest fear was that they'd overdose in an alley all alone. I knew I'd never be able to live with myself if that happened.

One Sunday, I was so frustrated I called the police to have them removed from my house. Ryan and Matt, driver's licenses in hand, waited patiently for the police. I didn't know that the law says that you cannot kick an adult out of their place of residence. They can be evicted, but you must fill out the proper paperwork, and that can take anywhere from forty-five to ninety days. The boys showed their driver's licenses to the cops, proving they lived with me.

The police officer lectured Ryan and Matt about how their drug use was affecting the family. Then he explained to me how to go about evicting them. After he left, I went to my bedroom and had a long cry.

Matt

On December 3, Katie invited us over for a birthday dinner in her honor. Everyone was going except Matt. I went to his bedroom to find out why. He was so incredibly high it was sickening. Matt very rarely displayed signs of being high. But he was not able to hide it this time. I feared he was close to overdosing. He told me he had used every bit of heroin that he had. He said he preferred dying than spending ten years in prison and that if he lived through the night, he'd accept his fate and just do the jail time. I told him that I was going to call 911, and he said he'd refuse the help, that he was an adult, and it was his right to do so. My heart broke. I didn't know what to do. He was right. If I called 911 and he refused treatment, there would be nothing I could do. I wanted to stay and watch over him, but if I didn't go to Katie's for her birthday, she'd be mad at me. I was always choosing her brothers over her, and that day, she was in no mood to hear another excuse.

I went over Katie's for about an hour. She said she was upset with Matt for not joining me, and I thought it was best if I didn't comment on his condition. When I got home, he was thankfully still alive. I continued to check on him throughout the night and thanked God that he made it through until morning. He packed a suitcase and checked himself into treatment. He has been clean and sober ever since.

Matt was discharged from treatment on December 18 so he wouldn't miss his court date for the sixty-four plus charges on December 21. Matt plead guilty on all the charges in hopes they would go harder or him than Ryan since he had a son to raise. Matt was due back in court on February 5 for his sentencing hearing.

Ryan

Ryan was trying to stay clean. He was attempting to go longer stretches of clean time with no maintenance drugs like Suboxone to assist him. Unlike the other times when Matt got clean, Ryan gave Matt his space so he could remain clean. He went out of his way to avoid Matt so he wouldn't be a trigger to cause a relapse. Ryan spent a lot of time at Katie's house. We all respected his effort.

Ryan's court date was scheduled for the first week in January. The week before, after meeting with Ryan privately, his attorney came to me and said it was imperative that he seek treatment immediately because it was the only way to lessen his charges. I agreed, but Ryan had no health insurance, so that was the first thing he needed to handle. Ryan asked me to take him to the Department of Social Services to apply for state insurance. Social services was practically empty that day, so we were in and out in no time. He was verbally approved for state health insurance. His card would arrive in about one month. I then drove Ryan to a local outpatient facility. Ryan was told they don't take walk-ins. He made an appointment for the following week. The next week, Ryan walked back to the local outpatient treatment center to apply for rehab. He had his intake session with a family member of owner of the treatment center. He told him to come for treatment when he had his insurance card in hand.

I attended court with Ryan. He told the judge and his attorney that he had pending treatment. Ryan was given eighteen months of supervised probation and told that he must get treatment. He told me later that he was finally ready to move forward. He was sick of his life—constantly using drugs and wondering where his next fix was coming from. He wanted a job and to be able to finally take care of his son.

Our family had a meeting about where to go from there. We knew Matt was going to jail. We just didn't know for how long. We were praying it wouldn't be for ten years. Ryan needed treatment and wanted to get out of Pasadena as soon as he completed the four-month outpatient treatment plan. Tim needed constant care and supervision. I wanted to get out of Pasadena too, but I needed to work, and I liked my job. I was fifty-eight years old and afraid to find a new job. We had a contract on the sale of the house, and if all went well, we'd be moving soon.

We all agreed that as soon as Ryan completed his four-month treatment, he was going to have his probation and parole changed to our home near the beach. He would care for his father while making a fresh start for himself. I got my work days grouped together. I worked three days in one week and four the next. While working, I would stay at Katie's house. On my days off, I would make the two-and-a-half-hour drive to join Ryan and Tim for a few days. It was the first time in years that we had a positive plan in place.

As January progressed, Ryan was finding it harder to remain sober. He was verbal about his struggles. On January 28, he said he would never make it another week without drugs. Ryan had to check in with his probation officer on January 29. I suggested that I take him to the meeting, and we could get breakfast beforehand. They were calling for an ice storm later that day, so I wanted to get on the road early.

We got on the road as planned. We hit up Starbucks, McDonald's, and the probation and parole office. Ryan was in a great mood that day, and it put me in a good mood as well. Ryan inquired about having his parole moved to the beach. His probation officer said the transfer could be arranged if he successfully completed his treatment. The probation officer said the move would be positive for him. Ryan beamed with positivity for his future. The last thing he said to me before getting out of the car when we got home was, "I love you, Mom. I can't wait to leave Pasadena. I'm never coming back." I told him I loved him too.

That was the last time I saw or spoke to Ryan. He died of a heroin overdose that afternoon. His income tax refund came that day. We knew he was struggling, and we assume that he wanted to get high one last time before getting clean. His father saw him on the front lawn around 3:00 p.m., and then he disappeared. His phone records show that he had called to confirm the IRS deposit. He then called two dealers. One called him back, and they met at the 7-Eleven down the street from us. He met the same dealer about an hour later for more heroin. I think he needed more because Matt had given Ryan a small piece of his Suboxone the day before. The Suboxone prevented him from getting high the first time, so he bought more. It was a fatal dose.

I found Ryan at 7:30 p.m. When I got home from work around 6:00 p.m., his room was dark and quiet. Usually, his light and TV were on. We assumed he was out with Katie's father-in-law shopping for supplies he needed for a repair job they were doing together. As it got later, the roads got worse due to the weather. I was worried because he wasn't back yet. I called his phone, and no answer. Then I called Katie to have her call her father-in-law to ask how much longer they'd be. She called me right back and said he had canceled due to the weather.

I went to Ryan's room in the basement and found him next to his bed. I screamed, and Matt came right away. I don't remember much because I was in shock. We called 911. My worst nightmare had come true. My baby boy was gone. He was so close to getting clean. I really thought we were going to come out of the dark times okay. Things will now never be the same. How was I supposed to live the rest of my life without Ryan? How was Ryan's son going to grow up without a father? Despite his addiction, Ryan really was becoming a great dad and never missed a chance to tell his son how much he loved him.

I was scared that Matt was going to relapse. Losing your best friend, who was also your twin brother, was an incredibly hard hit. Katie was also broken. She and Ryan spent so much time together. They were always planning activities together for the kids. Tim was void of feelings. His strokes destroyed the part of his brain that allow him to express emotion. He also suffered from short-term memory loss. We constantly had to remind him that Ryan was gone.

The very next day, I had to call the state's attorney's office. Matt's sentencing hearing was scheduled for the day after Ryan's funeral. I was to bury one son one day and watch the other be taken away in handcuffs the next. It was more than I could handle. The state's attorney was sympathetic. She told me not to worry about court and that she would contact the judge to request a postponement.

We got to see Ryan's body after it was released from the coroners and prior to cremation. He looked so handsome, like he was asleep. It was so hard seeing my baby lay there. But he looked like he was at peace. The service was overwhelming. People came out of the woodwork to support our family and pay their respects. Ryan thought he didn't have any friends, but the funeral home got so packed they had to start a single file line to usher everyone in. I hope Ryan was looking down on all the love that was sent to him that day.

After the funeral, I wanted a day without receiving people, but I was afraid of being alone with my thoughts.

With the sale of the house approaching, we had a tentative settlement date for early March. I decided to throw myself into packing up our belongings. Ryan's room was the hardest. I had to pack things I hadn't seen since he was a baby. Katie and Matt were mentally unable to help me. Ryan's son got really upset that I was packing his father's stuff. He was unpacking as quickly as I was packing. He said his daddy liked things the way they were and that I had no right to touch them. He was deeply hurting, and I didn't want to make things worse, so I packed up when he wasn't around. He asked me not to move because he felt like we'd be leaving his father behind. My heart was breaking. How do you make a six-year-old understand that his daddy's spirit was not being left behind even though his things were?

My feelings about the house and the area were different. I couldn't get out fast enough. I hated the house. I hate the area. The last ten years had been so painful. The house sucked the life out of my soul. I knew the longer we lived there, the longer it would take for me to heal.

Matt and I were notified of his rescheduled court date. I was assured by the state's attorney that everything would be okay and everyone was on Matt's side. He remained in outpatient treatment. He had every reason to relapse, but he stayed strong and sober.

As promised, everyone was on Matt's side. If he remained clean, he would be on a five-year extreme supervised probation. The judge, who was also a mother, said she found it difficult to take Matt away from me during such a difficult time. She also made it clear to Matt that she could change her mind if he messed up.

Matt found work despite his felony conviction. The company frequently hires recovering addicts. The owner said he was only giving Matt one chance, so he'd better not screw it up. I was happy for him but scared that a job might break him. This would be the first time in a long time that Matt would have money and freedom and time away from my constant watch. I told him I was scared, and he admitted that he was too. We both agreed that it would be best if I handled his money and drove him to and from work.

The sale of the house fell through. At the time, I thought it was a curse, but in time, I saw it as a blessing. I needed time after Ryan's death to come to terms with my house. I needed to lose ten years of hate and to remember and relive all the good memories. I needed to see that baby boy taking his first steps, to see him opening his birthday and Christmas gifts, to see him ride a bike for the first time, and to remember kissing his boo-boos. I needed to remember the ball games in the yard and roller blading down the street. I remembered him playing pranks on his siblings and him driving away in his first car. I not only needed to remember all the good about Ryan but Matt and Katie as well. My home and family were the most important thing to me. It took almost a year, but the good memories started to replace all the bad, except for Ryan's death, obviously. That will hurt forever.

Katie talked me into going to grief counseling, and I'm so thankful she did. For a couple of months, I only went to private sessions, but then I started going to group sessions. The group was comprised of parents who also had lost a child to heroin. It helped to grieve with them. Our stories were all so similar—years of missed opportunities, misdiagnoses, denied treatment, and in and out of the court system. We all felt shame from having a child as an addict. The shame that kept us all from reaching out to others until it was too late. We had all suffered in silence, and in group, we leaned on one another.

The group has given me the courage to speak out about addiction. I now have a voice and an opinion, and I plan to use it to make changes for addicts and their families.

Necessary Changes

1. *State Health Insurance*

Ryan should not have been told to come back in thirty days after getting insurance. With state insurance, the policy number is available to health-care providers approximately two days after verbal approval. It's also three months retroactive to receive payment for services rendered if the proper paperwork is filled out. I took that issue to my local government. The delegate to whom I spoke told me that he planned to make treatment facilities follow policy when it comes to state insurance. He said they would be held accountable for denying someone immediate treatment.

Ryan did not have to die. I will not rest until I know for a fact that this is a law.

2. *Treatment*

Most anyone who has had a family member in treatment can understand fourteen to twenty-eight days in treatment is not long enough. It's no more than a glorified detox. There is no cure for addiction. It is only treatable if someone is willing to work hard to manage it. Six months gives an addict a much better chance of not relapsing. The damage the drugs have done to the body and brain need extended time to heal. No insurance company would deny or limit a person with any other disease treatment. Why is addiction not treated the same way?

Mental health facilities need to accept that suicide is not the only mental health problem. Depression and bipolar need treatment too. Most suicidal patients have mental health issues that went unaddressed. It's been proven that addiction and mental health issues go hand in hand. It should be treated as such.

The cost for treatment needs to be more affordable. Most addicts have no money and cannot afford the cost to get better in a facility.

3. *Family Advocacy*

I believe a family member should be able to act as an advocate for someone suffering from addiction regardless of their age. Many addicts are not of sound mind and are not able to make sound decisions regarding their life. It's been proven that addiction destroys the part of the brain that controls decision-making, judgments, and emotions.

Judges, lawyers, and police officers make decisions on their behalf all the time. I am the mother. And I did not stop being the mother when they turned eighteen years old. I understand and respect that one needs to want treatment for it to work. Longer stays in rehab could make it work. I knew my child had a problem before he did. I knew my child had a problem when it would have been easier to treat. I knew there was a problem before it escalated to heroin. I knew there were mental health issues before addiction. I knew there was a problem before the law was broken. I knew there was a problem before my son died.

I truly respect the court system and how it works. But I think I could have saved everyone a lot of work and possibly saved Ryan's life and made Matt's a lot easier. I do not want to be denied rights as a parent.

4. *Treatment versus Jail Time*

Most states are moving in the direction of treatment instead of jail time. I hope all states eventually put this into policy. It makes sense, and it's less costly. Addicts are not bad people. They are people who need help, not punishment. Their poor decisions are due to the disease. I wish Matt would have been part of this direction. He wouldn't have a felony on his criminal record.

5. *Addictive Pain Medications*

Heroin has been around for years, so how did it escalate to epidemic proportions? I see one logical answer: the overprescribed and overuse of pain medication. The prescriptions aren't just for a few days. They are often prescribed for thirty days at a time. Matt was addicted in two months. I don't believe doctors are intentionally trying to get patients addicted to pain meds, but they have a responsibility when issuing these drugs to be more careful. They should cut back on the amounts they prescribe and limit refills. If they don't, they should have to face criminal charges. If they act like dealers, they should be punished as such.

Pain management centers are even more out of control than doctors. Opioid use was not initially intended for long-term use. Originally, it was intended for patients who were in their last stage of life to be made more comfortable until they passed away. Pain management centers really need much stricter regulations. Many drug dealers use these centers to obtain pills to sell on the street.

A common myth regarding opiates is that people don't overdose from them; they only overdose from heroin. That's not true. Opiates are a form of heroin, and it is certainly possible to overdose. Most heroin addicts were opiate addicts first. They switch to heroin because it's much cheaper and easier to get. Sadly enough, a heroin addict or family member of heroin addicts are less likely to speak out and ask for help because of the stigma associated with a heroin addiction. This needs to end. Addiction is addiction regardless of the choice of drug.

Moving Forward

I have cried every day for the past 16 months, 518 days. Some days it's a long, hard cry. Other days, it's a hard swallow and a single tear. Regardless, the pain is all the same. It's the most unbearable pain. I intend to use that pain to prevent others from ever feeling it.

Ryan's life wasn't defined by how he died but by the many wonderful years prior to his addiction. I will honor his life and memory by working toward improvements to the system that he and others were denied and suffered from consequently.

- Content by Denise Williams
- Edited and formatted by Erin Drew (eedrew@gmail.com)
- Published April 2017

Part 2

In part one, there were a few things that happened that will be repeated in part two—things that I may not have completely understood or didn't know the significance of what happened at the time. They will be repeated in part two with more detail.

I had hoped and prayed my family's story of addiction, mental health issues, and heartbreak would end with Ryan's passing. It did not. After losing Ryan, our family slowly moved forward. I wouldn't go as far as to say we were healing. No one ever heals from a loss so devastating. But we were all trying to find our new normal. One thing I can say, losing Ryan brought us closer together.

We all had our own way of dealing with the loss. I needed to see Ryan's face everywhere. I started displaying photos of him all over the house. This upset Katie and Matt. To them, it was a constant reminder of our loss. To me, it was including Ryan in everything we were doing. Katie didn't want to see his face, but she didn't mind talking about Ryan. Matt, on the other hand, didn't want to see Ryan's face or talk about him. Matt avoided everything that had to do with Ryan. He threw himself into his work and his recovery. The busier, the better.

Matt's work was a confidence builder for him. Matt was very knowledgeable about most remodeling and renovation work. He was very surprised to learn how much he didn't know. The challenge of learning new skills was good for Matt. Matt was always a quick learner, and his work was no different. Initially, Matt loved his job, and it showed. In no time at all, Matt's boss awarded him with a team and a company truck. Matt's job was really the only thing that kept him going.

In the evenings, Matt would attend an IOP (intensive outpatient) treatment for his addiction. It was at a local addiction counseling facility. He had been attending treatment there when Ryan passed. It was the same facility that denied Ryan treatment. Despite how we now felt about the facility, we both thought it was best for Matt if he continued his treatment there. Besides work and IOP, Matt had no life. He pretty much stayed to himself and would stay in bed when he was at home. He blamed himself for Ryan's death and often told us he didn't feel like he deserve to be happy or even live. Whenever we did something to remember or celebrate Ryan's life, Matt stayed away.

Ryan and Matt's thirtieth birthday was on April 28, three months after Ryan's passing. It was an especially hard day for all of us. How does one celebrate one twin while mourning the other? Matt felt especially guilty. He had always asked to have just one birthday all to himself. Just one birthday he didn't have to share with Ryan. He wished he had never asked for it. Karma—be careful of what you ask for. Now he would give anything to celebrate their birthday together again.

On the few occasions, when Matt did talk about Ryan, it was to say how concerned he was that he was not able to cry. It bothered him that his grief was so bottled up. He said he often had dreams or rather nightmares about Ryan. Ryan would come to him in a demon form as he slept. He said Ryan blamed him for his premature death.

I suggested that Matt get professional help. Matt refused. He said everyone grieves differently. He also thought he deserved to be suffering the way he was. I didn't want to push Matt. I was just so grateful to have a clean and sober Matt. I feared if I pushed too much, he might relapse. I prayed Matt would find peace within himself.

Me

In March of 2015 (weeks after Ryan's passing), our newly elected county executive Steve Schuh hosted a town hall meeting at the local community college. It was to discuss the county's growing opiate epidemic. It was a follow-up from his news broadcast that aired two days before Ryan passed away. At the news broadcast, Steve Schuh declared the epidemic a state of emergency.

The town hall panelist consisted of a recovering addict, a family member of an addict, a spokesperson from the health department, crisis center, a treatment center, and the local chief of police. Tim, Katie, me, and about four hundred angry and frustrated people attended.

Katie and I listened to the panelist in disbelief. We were squeezing hands while listening to what we believed to be all lies. Throughout the seven years of addiction in our house, we contacted each of them, begging for help. We were never once offered the help they were talking about.

When the panelist finished talking, the attendees were invited to join in the conversation. It seemed like most of the room got in line to speak. Katie was one of them. Everyone seemed to be as angry and frustrated as we were. It was apparent we weren't the only family who went looking for help and never got it. When it was Katie's turn to speak, she went right down the row of panelist and called each of them out. She especially went hard on the representative from the treatment center who claimed no one ever gets turned down for treatment who seeks it regardless if they have insurance or not. Katie briefed her on Ryan's story. She said he was turned away after he applied for insurance on his own. He was preapproved and still told to come back in thirty days.

The representative started out by saying something like, "You must keep in mind, we are a profit-seeking business and not a non-profit." Her statement did not go over well with the crowd. She went on to express her condolences to Katie. She said Ryan should have been offered a "bridge" until his insurance went into full effect. She did not explain what a "bridge" was.

We went there looking for answers but came home even more frustrated and angry the before. We also had more questions. What was a bridge? Why wasn't it offered to Ryan?

In mid spring, Katie encouraged me to seek grief counseling. Initially, she went with me. I talked mostly about Ryan (and Matt), but I also talked about all I had lost over the past several years. It was like the flood gates had opened, and I had a lot to say.

After attending a few months of private therapy, I started attending a group session—a small but rapidly growing group of parents all who lost a child to an overdose. It was apparent I wasn't alone with my anger. We all hit one brick wall after another, trying to get our children help. We all believed we were let down by the health-care system and society. It cost our precious baby's their lives. Everyone also admitted that because of the stigma surrounding addiction, we remained silent. We even remained silent on our personal suffering. Now we all belong to this exclusive club that no parent should ever have to belong to.

I felt connected to these people. I understood them, and they understood me. One mother who attended was very familiar to me, but I didn't know why. I tried to think of how I knew her but came up empty.

The first time I told Ryan's story, one mother said it's illegal to turn someone away from treatment unless there is no bed for them. I told her it was outpatient. She suggested I look further into it.

In late summer of 2015, after a group meeting, I was saying my goodbyes to everyone. The mother who was familiar to me mentioned said she had been on a news broadcast with County Executive

Steve Schuh last January when he declared the epidemic a state of emergency. She shared her son Lance's story on the broadcast.

I couldn't believe it. That's how I knew her. I saw that broadcast. It aired two days before Ryan's death. Ryan had been staying at Katie's house. He thought if he stayed over her house, he wouldn't trigger a relapse for Matt. Ryan came home looking for Matt. He was in very active withdraw. He was extremely ill and very agitated. Ryan was hoping Matt would spot him a few Suboxone or contact someone who could. Ryan would pay back the Suboxone the following week when he was finally in treatment. Matt was low himself and could only spot Ryan a half of a strip.

Ryan decided to stay and join us for dinner. We had the evening news on while we ate. The segment with the county executive and my friend from grief counseling Ann Youngblood came on. As Ann spoke about her son Lance, I cried. I truly felt as if I knew her. Every word she spoke hit me in the heart. I didn't know her, but I felt like I knew her pain. I couldn't stop crying.

Ryan, who was already agitated, said I was acting foolish. He reminded me that her son had passed away. Both of my sons were alive. Matt was doing great, and he would be in treatment in another week. Then he would also be fine. He assured me as he stormed out of the room, I would never have to know her pain. Ryan died two days later… I now know her pain firsthand.

Matt

Matt agreed to go away for the Fourth of July to the beach with us. We were going to join my sister Kathy at her beach house. While at her community resort pool, Matt ran into one of the directors of the outpatient center, who denied Ryan treatment. He told Matt he was very proud of him getting and staying clean. He expressed his sympathy on Ryan's passing. He told Matt he no longer worked at the facility. He left not long after Ryan's death. He said he also moved out of the area. He assured Matt he fought hard to get Ryan into treatment but was overruled. He said he quit because he couldn't work at a facility that put money over people's lives. He also said Ryan wasn't the only person that was turned away.

This was very hard to hear. Perhaps Ryan's story would have had a different ending had he not been denied treatment.

Matt successfully completed his IOP treatment at treatment center. The center refused to award Matt his certificate of completion. Matt didn't understand why. He was told by the girl at the front desk it was due to an outstanding balance of $65 owed to the center. Matt had insurance that paid 100 percent for his treatment, so what was the balance for? We were both confused. We both agreed it would be a cold day in hell before they got a penny from Matt.

Me

Even though I was going to grief counseling on a regular basis, I still felt like I was losing my mind. My anger was growing. It consumed me 24-7. I couldn't focus at work, home, or anywhere. I needed answers. Why did Ryan have to die? What was the "bridge" that Ryan should have been offered? Why hadn't the facility even contacted me to express their condolences? Did they even care about Ryan? I know they knew about Ryan's passing because Matt was still attending IOP when Ryan passed, not to mention Matt's conversation with the former director.

I know this might sound crazy, but I just kept thinking that years before when our dog passed away, I got a sympathy card from the veterinarian. Ryan was a human being whose passing deserved to be acknowledged.

One day, out of the clear blue, I decided I was going to the treatment facility to get my answers. When I arrived, I asked to speak to the owner of the facility. She was eating her lunch but agreed to see me. She said nothing to ease my mind in any way shape or form. She was extremely cold toward me. She never even said, "I'm sorry for your loss." She did acknowledge knowing who Ryan and Matt were, but nothing about Ryan's passing. She said she remembered Katie speaking at the town to hall earlier in the year and was touched at her story. She said she wondered which facility had turned Ryan away. She seemed caught off guard when she realized it was her own. Still she said nothing in the way of an apology. I was losing my cool and needed to leave. I left more upset than I was when I arrived. In fact, I was so upset I forgot to mention Matt and her director's conversation at the beach.

I continued talking to my friend Ann more and more. She was actively working toward making changes for suffering addicts and their families. I wanted to do that too. If I could make a change in even one person's life, maybe I wouldn't feel like Ryan's death wasn't in vain.

Ann occasionally spoke to parents of recovering addicts at a treatment center in Baltimore City called Mountain Manor. She started asking me to go along with her.

Ann shared her son Lance's story with the parents. She would then encourage and suggest things the parents should do once their loved ones were discharged. Things she didn't know to do when Lance was still alive. I was very impressed by Ann's strength.

When Ann was finished, there was still some time left, so the counselor asked me to share Ryan's story. I got to the part when the facility told Ryan to come back in thirty days when he had the insurance card. I was interrupted by one of the parents whose child was in treatment. The mother said her child came to Mountain Manor with no insurance and received treatment immediately. I was completely confused and at a loss for words while trying to process what the mother just said. Her child was not turned away or told to come back in about thirty days with an insurance card!

The counselor spoke up and asked me to continue. She said she would meet with me afterward to talk about the insurance issue. The counselor later told me Ryan should never have been turned away especially if he had been preapproved. There is a website for all health-care provider or treatment center who accepts state insurance—Medicaid. They can log on and get a patients group and identification numbers. The information is on the website about twenty-four hours after being approved, which means Ryan's insurance information had been posted for about a week when he went to the treatment facility. She also said Medicaid pays all insurance bills three months prior to being approved. She told me a lot of treatment centers and doctors don't follow the Medicaid guidelines because it's extra paperwork. She said she doesn't understand how any facility could turn an addict away for treatment when we all know it's such a small window of time you can help them before they use again. And as in Ryan's case, it was it might be their last time. I was jumping out of my skin with anger. Ryan *did not* need that insurance card to receive treatment!

I did try to seek legal counseling. I was told it would be very hard to prove. I also got the impression they were not willing to take a civil case due to the stigma surrounding addiction. The addicts know what they were doing and get what they deserved, even if it means death.

Ann and my friendship continued. We attended many events together. Ann had already been involved in fundraising to financially assist addicts with needed treatment and aftercare. Together we formed the Lance and Ryan fund, a nonprofit to help those struggling. Through our fundraising efforts, we have been able to pay partial co-pays for treatment, security deposits, and rent for sober living. We've been able to supply them with toiletries, etc. for their journey to a clean and healthy life. We also make ourselves available to their families to offer them support.

The support we've received from our families, friends, and community for our fundraising efforts have been overwhelming and humbling. Sadly, though for every one person we help, ten more reach out to us for help.

With the obvious need for treatment and education in our area, our county executive Steve Schuh appointed Nancy Schrum as head of constituent services. She was to work further with the community on the epidemic issue. She planned on hosting events with open communication, education, resource awareness, and change for the community.

Nancy named her program "Not My Child." She had a short film made in which she filmed and interviewed a few people and their families with real struggles. The film also included current statistics and facts regarding the epidemic. The film was shown as an introduction to every "Not My Child" panel discussion.

The panel consisted of pretty much the same people as the town hall a year ago. A family member who lost someone to an overdose, a young person in recovery, a representative from the health department, crisis response, state's attorney's office, treatment center, police and fire department.

I was asked to be part of the first one. It was held at Northeast Senior High School, the very school that Ryan, Matt, and Katie attended. It was the perfect location for me to be a panelist. Many of their old teachers still taught there and came out to support me. To my surprise, Ryan still held a track and field record at the school. It was very emotional for me.

I honestly wasn't expecting too much from the other panelist. I wasn't impressed at the town hall a year before and didn't think this was going to be any different. To my surprise, I couldn't have been more wrong. I was very impressed with the changes the county had made since that earlier town hall meeting. The ones in positions to make changes heard the cries of the people and reacted. I quickly formed bonds with the panelist. They were all good people who wanted change and were willing to do whatever it took to achieve it.

Ann and I were both asked to be a panelist on several occasions. Even if one or the other wasn't a panelist, we still attended as many discussions as possible. We found them to be very informative. I think I learned something new about the complicated disease of addiction each one I attended.

Nancy Schrum took me, Katie, Ann, and two other parents to our statehouse for the General Assembly Legislation 2016. We would be meeting our local delegate Nic Kipke. Nancy was hoping we would be able to give Nic valuable information and suggestions to get bills passed to combat the epidemic.

I spoke to Nic first. My suggestion was to not let treatment facilities to turn people away with pending insurance. He said that's already the policy for state insurance / Medicaid. I told him what happened to Ryan. He said Ryan never should have been turned away. If a facility accepts Medicaid, then they should have followed the guidelines and policies.

I ran into Delegate Nic Kipke about a year later. He told me he took Ryan's story to the legislation and got a bill passed in 2017.

Any caregiver or treatment center who accepts Medicaid and doesn't follow all the guidelines and policies *will* be held accountable.

Bill—Mgaleg.maryland.gov/2017RS/fnotes/bil-0009/hbl329. pdf. I just call it Ryan's law!

Another bill Nic Kipke tried to get passed was a bill allowing parents and other family members to act on behalf of an addict. The bill would give the family member the right to force the addict into treatment. The bill was passed but only for young adult children who are still covered by their parents health insurance plan.

Matt

Matt continued to believe his life was hollow and pointless. His top priority was to try to not think about Ryan. He occasionally dated or went out with friends. Every now and then, he would spend the weekend at Katie's house. They would watch movies, only wearing pajamas or comfy clothes and eat munchie type food all weekend. Matt really loved watching movies. This was one of his favorite pastime.

Matt was growing more and more discontent with his life. He was starting to lose interest in his job. He was distancing himself from everyone. He slept a lot. Matt was very open to Katie and me about his fear of his reoccurring dream of Ryan being a demon and blaming him for his death.

Even though Matt was obviously suffering, we talked frequently. He talked about his job, his life, his hopes, and fears. He listened while I did the same. We talked about our shared growing responsibilities for the care of his father who could be quite challenging at times.

Matt's probation officer often asked him to provide the court with his certification of completion from the treatment facility. Part of Matt's probation was to successfully complete the program. His probation officer was threatening to violate Matt if he didn't produce it. Matt told the officer what transpired at the treatment facility with his certificate. Matt really thought the probation officer didn't believe him. The officer decided to call the facility himself to get to the bottom of things.

Matt said the officer was on the phone with the facility for about twenty minutes before he came back to Matt and told him he could go to the facility and get it. The facility had agreed to release it.

Matt stopped by the facility on his way home. The same girl as before was at the front desk. As she handed Matt his certificate, she told Matt he must have misunderstood her before. She now said it was a $65 credit and not a debit. She said it was Ryan's credit, not his. She said she needed to know who was to receive the refund—him or me. She didn't want to release the certificate without issuing the refund.

I couldn't believe it. I was furious. Ryan had a $65 credit, and they turned him away. He could have used the money to start his treatment.

In June of 2016, while at work, Matt incurred a very serious eye injury. A coworker was using a grinder. Several metal wires flew across the room and landed up and down the right side of Matt's body. A two-inch dirty, rusty wire landed directly in the center of the cornea of Matt's eye.

Matt was sent to the Wilmer Eye Clinic at Johns Hopkins Hospital. He had quite a bit of damage done to his eye. The worst being he could have permanent damage. They cleaned the eye of several shard pieces of metal. They also needed to treat the infection that had already started forming. Matt was going to need surgery to replace the lens and repair a few tears after the infection cleared up. The surgery was scheduled for late summer, almost three months after the accident.

Matt was fired from his job. His boss claimed he was not performing his job at the same level he was hired. Wilmer Eye Clinic wanted Matt to be placed on light duties and no driving until after his surgery. His boss refused and fired him. It was a huge setback for Matt mentally. He was no longer happy at his job but had no intentions of quitting before finding another job. He was blindsided by the firing. With a pending surgery and not able to drive, Matt couldn't even look for work.

Matt was very honest and open with the medical staff at eye clinic about his past drug abuse history. Matt and I were both very nervous about the surgery. We were both aware an IV sedation could trigger a relapse. Matt came very close to opting out of the surgery. His doctor reassured Matt the sedation would be minimal and shouldn't trigger a relapse.

I drove Matt to the hospital the day of the surgery. Most of Matt's veins had collapsed due to years of IV drug use. The staff at the hospital had to call in a vein specialist to start his IV. The specialist came to Matt's cubicle with an intern. The specialist said out loud to his intern, "For some reason, Mr. Williams thought it was a good idea to stick needles into his veins, and now we are needed to fix things for him so he can have surgery."

I saw a complete look of embarrassment and shame on Matt's face. I wanted to speak out about his rudeness, but Matt gave me a look to keep my thoughts to myself. Matt thought I would make a bad situation worse by saying something. I sat there and quietly cried for Matt.

Matt made it through his surgery fine. He regained only part of his vision back. He continued to have light sensitivity. Matt needed a second operation but chose not to have it.

To this day, I still get so angry at the vein specialists poor bedside manner. How can we expect to educate the public on the disease of addiction when doctors who should be educated on the disease openly stigmatize a recovering addict? I've often wondered, did that doctor ever stop and think that so many of today's addicts first drug dealer wore a white jacket, has a stethoscope around their neck, and has MD after their names, just like him? He had no right to say what he did.

Matt said hearing comments like that is something he would have to deal with the rest of his life, so he might as well get used to it. Matt didn't relapse that day but claimed he had thoughts of using again because of how the vein specialists comment and the IV made him feel.

In the fall of 2016, Matt and I were asked to be part of a documentary film about the opiate epidemic in Anne Arundel County. It was a project for the University of Maryland film students. Two film students came to our house to interview us. The students also borrowed old family films and pictures for the documentary. The interview was raw, honest, and emotional, especially Matt's portion.

The film students presented the finished product to the public in early December. Matt's and my segment is titled "The Missing Half." It is heart-wrenching to say the least. Matt's pain over his own drug use and the guilt of Ryan's death is so incredibly painful to watch and hear. The interview was the first time Matt talked in length about Ryan. He was very honest and open. It was heartbreaking.

To view the documentary, google University of Maryland ViewFinder. Select ViewFinder Takes on the Heroin Crisis in 2016. Our portion was titled "The Missing Half." I was told later by the film student director that the documentary won awards for the students, and she thought our portion played a big role in it.

Matt continued to only exist and not truly live. He was very verbal about his depression and how much he hated going to sleep at night because of the Ryan demon who haunted his dreams.

Matt did find work with an old friend. Matt was also doing some side work for others.

Me

I continued to be obsessed with holding the facility accountable for Ryan's death. The very least I wanted them to acknowledge that Ryan should not had been denied treatment until his insurance card came.

I had requested to talk to the owner once again. I was promised she would call me by another staff member. After waiting several weeks for her to call, I decided to call her. She answered my call and said would call back as soon as she got Ryan and Matt's files. She did call me back after she got the files. She also put me on speaker and had a few staff members to join in the conversation.

It was obvious she was annoyed with having to speak to me. She started the conversation by asking me what I wanted from her. I told her I needed answers. I needed to know why Ryan was denied treatment until his insurance card came in when she could have gone on the website to get his group and identification numbers. She claimed she knew nothing about any website and if I was so concerned about Ryan getting immediate treatment when why didn't I go onto the website myself.

She said Ryan did come in seeking treatment. He was told they don't accept walk-ins, so he stormed out. I reminded her Ryan may have been upset, but he did make an appointment for the following week before storming out. He returned and had his intake interview with her director, but someone with more authority than her director still denied him. She then acknowledged Ryan did talk to her director, but it wasn't for his intake interview. Her director was not a certified clinician and could not do intake interviews.

She said it was her decision to turn Ryan away until his insurance card came because he never completed his treatment in 2013 and another time years before that. I knew about the 2013 time, but not the earlier time. I asked her about the $65 credit Ryan had. She said he didn't have credit. It was a payment from Medicaid for his 2013 treatment. It just happened to take Medicaid over two years to pay that claim.

It was her and her staff against me. I hung up still without hearing, "I'm sorry for your loss." Her explanation that Ryan was turned away because he didn't complete the program in the past was bogus. Matt was treated there so many times—many more times than Ryan ever was. In fact, the first time Matt ever successfully completed his treatment was this last time. Matt was never once denied treatment.

Someone recommended that I contact this company who investigates local businesses who might not be operating on the up and up. The representative from the company did go to the treatment facility. She spent hours there going through their books and Ryan and Matt's files. She said she didn't find anything huge. There were a few issues, but not enough to violate them or shut them down. She said Ryan and Matt's files were a mess. Some of Ryan's data was in Matt's file and vice versa. She said there was nothing in Ryan's file to indicate he was there in December of 2014 or in January of 2015. She did not see anything in Ryan's file that the $65 payment from Medicaid could be posted too.

The representative told me she wasn't at liberty to do anything that would overstep her authority. She did suggest I consider contacting Ryan's insurance company. She refused to elaborate on why or what I was to look or ask for. I racked my brain for days before I came up with possible insurance fraud. Did the facility place a claim to Medicaid for treatment Ryan never received? What else could it be?

I still had the envelope with Ryan's insurance card and packet. It came the day of Ryan's funeral. I never opened it. The packet was like a knife in my heart. I examined his insurance card and noticed the day his insurance went into full effect. It was January 26, 2015, three days before Ryan overdosed. That knife just dug a little deeper.

I called the 800 number on the card. I explained to the representative what I was trying to do. She said, first, I had to prove I was

Ryan's next of kin. I had to mail her copies of Ryan's birth and death certificates and photo IDs for both of us. That took about two weeks before anyone from Medicaid could talk to me.

I was told Ryan's file stated he had applied for insurance on December 29, 2014, and was preapproved for immediate treatment. The very next day, his ID and group numbers were posted to the website. She said Ryan must have really pleaded his case to the social worker who helped him apply for insurance because it was noted in his application, "NEEDS IMMEDIATE TREATMENT."

She said the facility should have gone onto the website to get his group and ID number. She said if they accept Medicaid patients, then they should have known about the website. She didn't see any claims paid for Ryan for $65 in 2015 or in 2013. She also said it did not take years for Medicaid to pay a claim. She said only health-care providers and treatment have access to the website. I guess I'll never know why the facility received a payment for Ryan in the spring of 2015 for $65. I also never received a refund for the money from the facility like the girl at the front desk told Matt we were supposed to get.

Matt

In March of 2017, Matt was out of Suboxone. He called around, asking if he could buy one off anyone. He had plans that night and didn't feel comfortable going out without the safety net of a Suboxone. One of Matt's friends said he couldn't help him but knew someone who could. Matt agreed to go to her house to get it. As it turned out, this was one of the worst decisions Matt ever made. When Matt arrived at the house, there were other drugs being used. Matt not only relapsed, but he went on a five-day binge. For five days, Matt stayed in one crack house after another using.

Katie and I reported Matt missing after twenty-four hours. We felt because of Matt's past drug abuse history, the police weren't taking Matt missing serious. They had no intention of looking for him. To them, he was just another "junkie" on the street.

Katie and I decided it was up to us to find Matt. We knew he was at a very high risk of overdosing since he had been clean for over two years. We also knew that Matt might not want to be found.

I had a tracking devise on his phone. We tracked him to one of the worst parts of the city. When we saw him, I jumped out of the car and approached him. He took off and turned his phone off. We started leaving voice messages on his phone in hopes he would hear them and come home. My first message to him was not a nice one. I immediately regretted it. It was full of anger and rage. I said the type of things I knew you should never say to anyone who is suffering. I had no way of taking it back and hoped he would never hear it. All our messages after that were to tell him how much we loved him and just wanted him to come home.

Katie, Tim, and I would drive through the streets near where we tracked his phone to looking for any sign of Matt. We saw his car in front of what looked like a broken-down, rat-infested, abandoned house. We watched the house for days, waiting for Matt to show up.

On the fifth day after he disappeared, I got the phone call I had been waiting for. It was Matt wanting help. He wanted me to come get him. He sounded awful. He said he was ill and didn't know where he was. I told him to stay right where he was. I would track him with the app on my phone. I called Katie and told her to call 911 and send the paramedics to the house where Matt's car had been parked. I told her I was driving there to meet Matt and I would see her and Tim at the hospital.

The paramedics found Matt several blocks away from the place where we saw his car. They rushed him to the hospital for an apparent overdose. As I was getting ready to head to the hospital to be with Matt, two girls pulled up in his car. They told me Matt had given them his car. I called the police to help me get it back. The girls gave the keys back to me after the police got there. They also told me I should show them a little more gratitude since they were the ones who administered Narcan to Matt when he overdosed. I half-heartedly thanked them as I reminded them that they shouldn't have let Matt run off after they administered the Narcan. If they had been trained properly on Narcan, they would have known that.

I decided to leave my car there and drive Matt's car to the hospital. Katie and Tim were already there. Matt was really in bad shape. He was in active and violent withdrawal. The staff let us see Matt before they put him into a medical-induced coma to calm him down.

Matt remained in the hospital for several days. I called my friends from crisis response for help. I could never say enough good things about them. They came out of their jurisdiction to help us. The clinicians sat with me all day. They applied for and got Matt new health insurance that had lapsed since completing his IOP program. They had seen the documentary we made and said what happened to Matt was more of a mental health issue. His pain was so apparent in the film. She insisted he be treated as mental health issues rather than addiction.

Matt was transferred to the hospital's behavior health unit. He was treated there for an additional two weeks. After that, he would be treated in their outpatient program for as long as was needed.

In the behavior health unit, I briefed one of the staff members on what happened. She was more interested in the fact that Matt had a twin brother who died—a death that Matt felt responsible for than that he had relapsed and overdosed. She told me she had done some research on twins. The study showed that twins are one. They have a greater bond than even a mother and child. Losing a twin sibling is like losing a part of oneself. It's like what losing a body part would be to us. It's a form of PTSD.

I found what she said next really disturbing. She said it's not uncommon when one twin passes away, the surviving twin will find a way to reunite with their twin within five years. Sometimes it's intentional. Sometimes they become unconsciously reckless with their lives until they pass away too. She wasn't concerned that Matt had relapsed but was surprised it took so long to do. Matt is a twin who has never dealt with his guilt or grief. It was never if he would relapse but when. Matt was like a volcano waiting to erupt, and when he did, he handled it the only way he knew how—to use again or, rather, self-medicate.

Wow, that was really a lot to take in. The five-year thing made me sick to my stomach. Two years had already passed since Ryan died. If what she said was true and Matt didn't get the help he needed, we might only have three more years with Matt. I knew I would never survive losing Matt too.

Not long after Matt was discharged from inpatient treatment, he relapsed again. He went back to the same crack house as before. This time, I wasn't going to wait for Matt to call; I was going after him. I went to the house and knocked on the door. I told the person who answered the door if he didn't send Matt out immediately that I was going to call the police and report that the occupants in the house stole my car. I pointed to Matt's car and told the person it was my car and not Matt's. He asked me to wait a minute while he went to get Matt. Matt came out. He looked terrible and started vomiting. After we talked for a few minutes, Matt agreed to come home.

Matt went back into treatment. Over the next nine months, Matt was in three different mental health inpatient and outpatient treatment facilities. One time, it was for a serious allergic reaction to one of his antidepressants. It was, of course, a huge setback to his recovery. Finding the right medication and making sure it works correctly with the other medication can be difficult.

I stayed in close contact with all his doctors, therapist, and counselors. I was determined I was going to do everything in my power to help Matt. Together we would get through this. Matt wasn't very convinced he would get better. Matt claimed Ryan was still coming to him in his dreams as a demon and blaming Matt for his death.

In addition to everything Matt was dealing with within himself, we had a neighbor who was constantly harassing Matt. This had been going on for over a year. The things he was doing to Matt was making him even more depressed. It was totally uncalled for and unprovoked. A couple of the other neighbors who had been aware of what was being done to Matt asked the harassing neighbor to stop. His response to one of them was "Once a junkie always a junkie." He never stopped harassing Matt.

We all noticed Matt was off. He was really struggling to stay afloat. We all suggested Matt talk to his doctor about what was going on. Matt didn't want to call her. He thought if he called her, she would just increase his medication. Matt thought the dosages were already too high for him. They made him feel like a zombie and want to sleep a lot. He also thought they weren't taking his depression and anxiety away.

I went with Matt to his January 2018 doctor's visit. I wanted to personally talk to his doctor. I didn't trust that Matt would be completely honest with her. I didn't get to privately talk to her, but she did come out to the waiting room to ask that I make sure Matt get blood work done before his next visit.

Matt must have really been honest with her. Not only did she order blood work, but she also wanted to see him back in one month instead in three months. Matt was probably right about her increasing his medication. The blood work would show if his levels were off.

If they were, she planned on adjusting the amounts—in other words, increase them.

Matt asked Katie and Josh if they wanted to have "movie" weekend. It's a weekend where everyone stays in their pajamas or comfy clothes all weekend. We eat lots of junk food and watch movie after movie. We all loved these weekends every now and then.

Matt packed his weekend bag and headed to Katie and Josh's house. Matt came back before the weekend was over. His frame of mind was worse than it was before. He refused to talk about it.

Katie told me she didn't think the weekend went well at all. She said after she and Josh went to bed, they heard Matt going through a drawer of an end table on their middle level. Matt slept on their lower level, so there was no reason for him to be on the middle level. They both thought he was acting suspicious. He was either hiding drugs or looking for something to pawn. Josh searched the end table drawer that Matt was going through. He found nothing. The drawer was full of their kids' saved schoolwork papers. Katie and Josh made Matt go back to the lower level. They put the baby monitor on him so they could monitor his movements.

Matt continued to be more and more depressed.

On February 13, 2018, Matt had his workmen's compensation hearing for his eye injury. Matt's lawyer was also planning on trying to recover some compensation from his car accident in 2007. I went with Matt to the hearing. Part of his lawyer's strategy was to bring up Matt's past drug and criminal history before the opposing lawyer did. I silently cried as Matt sat on the witness stand with his head down. Matt acknowledged that the drug-using, law-braking person his lawyer was describing was him. It was heartbreaking.

On the drive home, Matt said the person the lawyer described didn't deserve to live. He was an awful person who needed to die. I tried to convince Matt what was said in court was just strategy. His past was not as bad as the lawyer described. He challenged me to name one thing that was said that wasn't true. I couldn't but told Matt what was said was exaggerated. I know Matt saw right through me. The hearing was brutal and painful.

The next couple of days with Matt were extremely difficult. Each one of us knew Matt was off and acting out of character. Regretfully, we didn't talk about it with each other.

February 14
Tim and Matt

Matt went to Tim. Matt held his father's hand. He told him he was sorry for all the terrible things he had down over the past several years. Tim said Matt kissed his hand and told him he loved him.

February 15
Katie and Matt

Matt and Katie went to pick up a TV for me. Matt told Katie if he got any money from his hearing, she was to see that Ryan's son and her sons were taken care of. She asked Matt if she should be concerned about him. He told her no and asked her not to tell me about the conversation because I would be worried.

February 15
Katie's View

Matt and I decided to buy our mom a new TV and stand. My mom always did so much for us, and we wanted to do something for her in return. I came over to pick Matt up. After we were in the car and ready to leave, Matt told me he forgot something and needed to run back inside. I waited in my car for a solid ten minutes; these ten minutes felt more like fifteen to twenty minutes. I decided to go check on Matt and see what was holding him up. I walked across the front lawn to just peek in Matt's window. I noticed he was smoking something. Matt and my eyes met.

I said to him while tapping on the window. "Come on. What's taking you so long? Let's go!"

Matt said, "Okay. I'm coming."

I knew what Matt was smoking; it was crack cocaine. Matt knew I knew what he was smoking, but it was supposed to be a good night for us and mainly for our mom. I didn't want to start another big fight over drugs. I turned a blind eye like I did, only too often, when trying to keep the peace. When Matt got back into the car, Matt immediately started talking. I'm sure he did this to try and distract me from what he knew I had seen. Matt was very hyper, talking extremely fast, and was very happy. These were all things Matt was normally was not. Matt was telling me about what happened at court earlier that week. He was upset about how he was portrayed that day but, at the same time, grateful for his lawyer because he felt like he won and would finally be able to financially help with bills. Matt wanted to do some major necessary work on our parents' house and would be able to give me money toward my boys for college. He disclosed with me that he always felt like he should have been the one to step up with Ryan's son. He was his godfather and Ryan's twin. To him, that meant he should have been the father figure in his life.

I said, "Matt, don't feel that way. I have been taking good care of him, and he feels a sense of family with us. You have your own burdens and demons that need to be addressed first. That little boy is in good hands with us."

Matt continued to talk about that money he was potentially getting. Matt said he needed to tell me something but was afraid if he did, I would take it the wrong way and go to mom with the information. I promised Matt I wouldn't. That if he had something to tell me, I would keep it between us, that I didn't always tell mom everything we talked about. Matt believed me, and then told me that if he won his case, I was to make sure the money was divided up like so. Half was to go to my mom, a few thousand was to go to me and my husband—to pay back for all the things he stole over the years—some was to go to my aunt, for all the help she gave to him over the years, and the remainder was to be divided up between my three children and Ryan's son—with more going to Ryan's son since he didn't have a father and could use more financial help. I was confused when he broke the money down this way. I thought to myself, *Okay, you covered this person and that person and payed back this person, but what about you? What about Matt.*

I looked over to Matt and stated, "Wow, Matt, that's generous, but you forgot about yourself. Matt, this is your opportunity to get ahead, to start over. You should use this money to get yourself the proper help you need, with the right doctor that fits you. Do some of the home improvements you wanted to do, buy your way into mom and dad's house. Shit, buy a new house. Matt, I know you want to give everyone a piece of the pie because you feel like it's your way to right your wrongs, but we all love you and just want you to take advantage of this, and use it for you. You must leave something for you."

Matt looked back at me, and with a strange face, said, "Oh yeah, well, I'll take some too."

I could tell he didn't mean what he said. I knew something wasn't right about this. We sat in silence for a minute, while I processed what was just said. When we came to a red light, I looked Matt straight in the eyes and said, "Matt, should I be worried? You've just given away one hundred thousand dollars and not left a dime for yourself and asked me not to tell mom about this conversation. I feel like I should be worried. Are you planning on killing yourself any time soon? I know you've been super down and haven't felt like you in a long time. I know that Ryan haunts you in your dreams, and you've always said you wish you were dead. You're scaring me."

Matt looked back at me with a big smile and giggled. "No, Katie, I am not planning anything. I'm just trying to right my wrongs like you said. I don't want you telling mom because she would overreact just like you are doing right now."

I said, "Okay, just promise me you'll keep some money for Matt, and you'll put some of toward bettering your health."

The rest of the car ride was a lighter topic. We picked up the TV and stand, drove home, and decided we would meet up Saturday morning to get it all set up for mom.

I knew in my heart there was more to Matt's words. As heavy of a conversation that Matt and I had, I kept my promise. I never told our Mother what was said between us that night.

February 16
My parents and Matt

I told Matt I was going to visit my parents. Matt told me he was going with me because he really needed to see and talk to them. Matt canceled with me at the last minute. While I was visiting them, Matt called them four times. He told them how much he loved them and how sorry was for all the bad things he did and put them through. This was very odd. Matt never called his grandparents, let alone call them four times in two hours.

February 17
Told by Katie

As previously planned, I came over on Saturday morning to put the TV and stand together for mom. Not surprising, Matt was still in bed, sleeping, when I arrived. I had three young children with me and a newborn baby. I was on a mission to get in and get out. Matt being his slow lazy self that morning was not going to cut it. I told Matt to get up and get moving. While waiting on Matt, I started assembling. I got to a point when I realized I needed his help. I went back into his room, only to find he had not moved at all. I started yelling at Matt. I was being very pushy with him. I needed to get the job done. Matt finally sat up and told me to come back; we would do it later. This infuriated me. I was *not* coming back. I needed it to be done right then and there. Matt got extremely agitated with me. Something that was out of character for him. It was nothing for me to yell and carry on, but for Matt to fight back, something was wrong. I called Matt out on the drug use I saw the night when we picked up the TV. That got Matt even more upset. It turned into a giant fight. It was obvious nothing was getting done with the TV. I packed my kids up and stormed out of the house. A few hours after I calmed down, I sent Matt a text. I apologized for the fight and my part in it. I knew Matt was really going through something. The last thing I wanted was for him to use again because of the fight we were having. I asked him to call me back when he could. Unbeknownst to me, this text was the last text message I would ever send my brother.

Around dinnertime, that same day, my phone rang. It was my mom. When I answered, I was surprised to hear Matt's voice. We talked about the fight that had transpired earlier that day. We both apologized for the horrible words we used and our actions. Matt asked me to come over the next day. It would be a Sunday. I reminded him that I always come over Sunday for dinner. He told me that he needed me to come over first thing in the morning. He needed to see the boys and me. He made me promise with everything in me that I would come over the minute I woke up. I promised and reassured him. We both apologized again. We both said I love you before hanging up. I remember getting off the phone with Matt and saying to my husband that Matt sounds uncommonly calm. I would figure out why the next day when I saw him.

February 17
Me and Matt

Matt had been up most of the night before. He was very loud and noisy, so I confronted him. He said he was having a hard time sleeping, so he decided to clean his room. I was very suspicious because it reminded me of the nights when he was using. I checked his room, but there was nothing out of place. Something was off, so I kept my eyes on him. Around dinnertime, I heard the front door open and shut. I got to the door to see Matt pulling away in his work van. I immediately call his cell phone. He didn't answer, so I left a voice mail. I threatened if he didn't come back right now, I was going to call his boss. I was going to tell him Matt was probably using the van to do a drug run.

Matt came back about forty-five minutes later. He said he went to get a pack of cigarettes and ran into someone he knew. I checked him for drugs but found none. He did have a new pack of cigarettes and a receipt. I asked him what was going on with him. He started crying. He sounded so broken and vulnerable. He told me it was time for me accept enough was enough. He could no longer live with or without drugs. He said he really tried to get better. It was time to accept he never would. I started crying too. He asked me to just let him go so he could find peace. He said he would never be able to forgive himself for Ryan. Matt said it was hard living with himself, knowing others would never forgive or forget his past. I said, "That's not true. No one is holding your past against you. Everyone loves you and supports you."

Matt pointed to the harassing neighbor's house. He said he reminds me about my past every chance he gets. I tried to reason with Matt and said he's a jerk. His opinion doesn't count. I begged Matt to go to the hospital. He said no but would go on Monday. He didn't want to have to sit in a hospital cubicle for a day and a half waiting for an evaluation. I asked him if he got the blood work done. He told me no, and he had no intention of getting it done either. He could hardly function with his medication the way it was and would not agree to it being increased. I asked him again to either go to the hospital or let me call crisis response. He wouldn't agree. The current law states if a person is over the age of eighteen and is not violent, no one, including their next of kin, can speak on their behalf. This law *needs* to change. I should have been able to call for help.

I took his phone and the work van keys from him. He hugged and kissed me and told me how much he loved me. He apologized for everything he put me through. He told me I was a good mother who did everything right. He asked me not to tell Katie about what happened because she would just overreact to everything. He hugged me again and went to his room.

February 18
Me

Matt was once again noisy and up all night. I mentioned it to him when he came out his room. Matt verbally attacked me, saying he didn't want to hear it. He was tired because he didn't sleep well and didn't need me nagging him. I told him I didn't deserve his attack. I wasn't nagging him. I simply said he was noisy and kept me up. He apologized right away, saying I was right and didn't deserve the way he was acting. He hugged me and went back to his room.

A couple of hours later, Katie and the boys were at the house. She said Matt had called her and asked her to bring the boys over. He wanted to see them. She agreed since she planned on cutting mine and her father's hair that day. I just assumed he wanted to see his nephews because he was going into treatment the next day, and it could be a month before he saw them again.

Katie went right to Matt's room. She said he was sitting on the edge of his bed in a daze. She asked what was wrong and if he had been up all night. She said he answered her with an attitude. She said her one son Zac came into the room and jumped on Matt. Matt hugged and kissed him. They talked for a minute or two. As Katie was leaving, she told Zac to, "tell Uncle Matt you love him and give him the biggest hug ever because it looks like he needed it." Katie gave Matt a hug and kiss and told him she loved him. She reassured him things would get better and left.

About fifteen minutes after Katie left Matt's room, she asked me to go check on him. She said she had never seen Matt as low as he was when she was with him. She said she was very worried about him. The door to his room was locked. I yelled to Katie for help. We got the door opened. We found Matt unresponsive on his bathroom floor. I called 911 as Katie administered Narcan and CPR. She said she was sure she heard him take his last breath. She was sure she broke his ribs while doing CPR.

February 18
Told by Katie

Sunday morning, I woke up, packed up a few things along with the boys, and headed over to my parent's house. When I walked in, I talked to my parents for a few minutes about the day before. I told them to get themselves ready because after I talked to Matt, I was going to color and cut their hair. I went down to Matt's room. When I walked in, Matt was sitting on the edge of his bed. I have never seen him look like this before. It was an empty shell. A hallow body. I walked over to him and asked if he had been up all night because he looked rough. With an attitude, Matt said back that he had, but he didn't want to hear it. I told him I would stay off his back and this is not why I came over. I brought up the day before and how he had wanted us to come over. He told me after he got himself up and more together, he would come out of his room, and we could talk. That's when my son Zachary came in the room. Zachary, only being five years old at the time, didn't understand that Matt needed a minute. He ran over and jumped on Matt's bed. I called for Zac and told him Uncle Matt just woke up and needed a minute before he could play with him. I told Zac to give Uncle Matt a big hug and tell him how much he loves him. I wanted to give Matt a minute to wake up. Before walking out of Matt's room, I reminded Matt that I loved him so much, and we would get through anything together as a family.

I walked back upstairs and started mixing the hair color for my mom. My mother and I talked more about the day before, and the fight that went down. I apologized for not having the TV together for her but reassured her it would be taken care of. After I finished putting the color on her roots, I immediately started on cutting my father's hair. About five minutes into the haircut, I wanted to go check on Matt. I was going to offer him a haircut too. I walked back down to his room, and I noticed he was in the bathroom. The bathroom door was shut and locked. I could hear the lighter clicking through the door. My head dropped in sorrow, knowing he was in his bathroom, getting high. I made a conscious decision to walk away from him. I was so mad, but that weekend had seemed so long, with all that had gone down. I honestly thought to myself, *Can't stop him anyway. He's going to do what he wants to do*. I walked back upstairs and continued cutting my father's hair. As heavy of a conversation that Matt and I had, I kept my promise. It was a matter of seconds when something clicked in, and I changed my mind. In true Katie fashion, I started yelling and carrying on. I was rambling about what Matt was down in his room doing and yelled for my mom.

I told her, "Matt is downstairs, in his room, getting high right now. If you don't go down and do something about it, I will."

My mom seemed annoyed with the way I went about it, but she marched right downstairs to Matt. I walked over to the top of the stairs to listen to what she was going to say to him and to be there for backup. I heard her knock on the door. I heard her knock again. This time with more force. Then I heard her call out to Matt. I knew in that moment and the way she said "Matt" what was going on. It was the moment we had been dreading for ten years. I rushed to her side to help. When I got down to Matt's room, my mom was trying to kick the door down. I knew she wasn't strong enough to do it, so I pushed her out of the way and called for Ryan's son. I told him to go outside and find me a brick and directed my mom to get me a screwdriver. When Ryan's son came back, I had already got the door open. I gave him my phone and told him to call 911. He told me he didn't know how. I grabbed my phone back and did it myself and handed it back to him and told him to wait for my instruction. Just then, my mom came back in the room and took the phone from Ryan's son. I immediately started CPR and told my mom to go grab the Narcan. I instructed Ryan's son to go grab up all the kids and baby and go to a room and shut and lock the door. That he was to take care of them and distract them from what was happening. I instructed him to not let any of them back downstairs no matter what until I say.

After my mom got me the Narcan, she went into a panic. Could I blame her? This was déjà vu. We were just here three years and twenty days before this. Everything was in slow motion. I continued CPR until the paramedics arrived. I remember them pulling me off from my naked brother's dead body. They slid him across the floor and started doing what they needed to do to try to save him.

I was screaming out, "I broke his ribs! I broke his ribs! I felt him take his last breath!"

One of the paramedics grabbed me and walked me out of the room, reminding me that that room was now a crime scene, and reassuring me that they will do everything they can. As we waked back upstairs, my mom was sitting in a chair in the corner with her color still in her hair, screaming and hitting the chair's arms. "Fuck, fuck, fuck! Goddamn it, Matt," with tears running down her face.

I looked over to see my dad pacing, screaming, "No, this can't be, Matt. This just can't be!"

The paramedic kept talking to me, but I had to excuse myself because I had four kids locked in a room upstairs who I needed to attend to. I could hear the baby crying. I made him a bottle and took it in to Ryan's son and asked him to stay put and to feed the baby. I told him I was going to call his mom to come pick them all up.

When I got ahold of his mother, I simply said as calm as I could, "Don't say a word. I don't have time to talk. I need you to listen carefully. Matt just overdosed. He's dead. They're still working on him, but I know he's dead. I need you to come over here right now and pick up all the kids and keep them until further notice."

She did exactly what I asked her. I packed the baby a diaper bag. By the time I was done, she was there. After the kids left, I knew I could give the paramedics the attention they needed, and my mom the attention she needed. I realized in that moment I had not yet cried. My heart was racing faster than I ever felt. It took about twenty minutes before they pronounced Matt legally dead. I don't know how to explain this but, as I cried when they officially said the words, it was like a sense of peace came over me. This is what Matt needed all along. Matt was planning this. Matt was at peace.

I arrived at my parent's house around 10:15 a.m. Matt was pronounced dead at 12:05 p.m.

Me

I thought I was going to get sick while waiting for the paramedics. They worked on Matt for about a half hour before they pronounced him dead.

I couldn't believe it—three years and twenty days later, my other baby boy gone. He was the most beautiful baby I had ever seen. His face was flawless with eyelashes that went halfway down his face when he closed his eyes. Matt had an angelic look about him. He was kind, smart, easygoing, and always eager to please. Everyone's best friend. And now he was gone.

It's so unfair that three years and twenty days after losing Ryan, we lost Matt. Katie and I both feel like it was an intentional overdose. We felt like Matt never saw himself getting better. He was a prisoner to his *depression and saw no way of breaking away from it. He was also a prisoner to his guilt over Ryan.* We do think Matt deserved to find inner peace. It just sucks that he found it at the expense of our hearts breaking further.

The next week was like moving in a fog. Only this time, we knew what needed to be done since we had been in this same place three years and twenty days before.

We did find a moment of peace the morning after. We saw two male cardinals flying back and forth across our yard. They appeared to be playing and chasing each other. We were aware of the tale that your angel is near when a cardinal appears. We saw two cardinals, and they were both males. We would like to believe it symbolized Ryan and Matt, telling us they were reunited and happy.

That same morning, I got a call from Matt's lawyer. Matt had won his workmen's compensation case. He was awarded $112,000. His lawyer thought since Matt was deceased and had no children, the case would probably be dismissed.

The local county TV station did a tribute to Matt (and Ryan). It included our portion of the documentary. I heard it was touching and heartbreaking at the same time.

Just like with Ryan, family and friends came out of the wood-work to pay their respects to Matt. The love and support shown to us was overwhelming. So many old friends were telling us the best stories about both boys. I could have listened to them forever. There is no question in my mind that my sons, Ryan and Matt, were loved and admired by so many people. I just wished they thought so too.

Matt's autopsy results came back that Matt had cocaine and fentanyl in his system. This was no surprise. What was shocking was, Matt suffered a massive heart attack. I probably shouldn't have been surprised. When I found Ryan, his eyes closed like he just went to sleep. Matt's were wide open and had a look of shock. Matt had attempted suicide several times over the years but always changed his mind and reached out for help. Would he have changed his mind and reached out for help this time but the heart attack prevented him from doing so? I'll never know.

In the spring of 2018, Katie was cleaning out the drawer of the end table that Josh found Matt going through. Stuffed in the middle the kids' school papers was a letter from Matt. It appeared to be the beginning of suicide note. It looked like he had started to write it when he was interrupted or stopped. Katie said she had cleaned out the drawer in November of 2017. It was not there then. That movie weekend in January was the only time Matt was in Katie's in 2018. It would make perfect sense that if Josh walked in on Matt writing a suicide note, he would have tried to hide it there.

Months after Matt's passing the dealer who sold Matt the deadly drugs was arrested and sentenced to jail. In January of 2020, Ryan's dealer was also sentenced to jail.

The neighbor who was harassing Matt continued to harass our family for a short time after Matt's passing.

We were awarded a small portion of Matt's workmen's compensation case settlement.

Tim started kidney dialysis in the summer of 2018. A few months later, he started having seizures and had to be put into a medical-induced coma for a couple of weeks. His health continues to deteriorate. Tim's health issues are a direct result of untreated high blood pressure.

Regrets and Missed Opportunities

I constantly look back over the past years and wonder what one thing could have changed our outcome. My answer is, never one thing but many things, especially three main ones.

The first thing happened when the boys were in high school just before graduation. Matt came to me with a letter from his English teacher. She asked me to contact her regarding a paper Matt had written. The assignment was for each student to write a speech. They were to pretend they were their class valedictorian. The speech topic was what would you say to or wish for their fellow classmates after graduation. Matt's speech was the most horrifying, disturbing, and mortifying paper I have ever read. He wrote about wanting to commit suicide, hating life, and not wanting to live in a world of evil.

My first thought was Matt didn't write the paper. It had to be either someone else wrote it and signed Matt's name to it, or it was his senior prank. He was happy-go-lucky and didn't have those types of feelings or thoughts. Or so I thought at the time.

Matt confirmed he did write the paper. It was no prank and was how he felt at times. Matt said he had those feelings more in middle school than high school. I asked him why he never said anything on how he felt. He said he was afraid to disappoint me and didn't want me to call him crazy like I often did to his grandmother. Tim's mother lived with us. She suffered from depression. I didn't understand nor did I try to understand how she felt. To me, she was a narcissist who was lazy and wanted attention. I thought if she would get out of bed, shower, and eat a good breakfast, her depression would go away. I was very verbal on how I felt. I asked Matt if he needed to see or talk to a psychiatrist. He said no, and he didn't have those feelings as much as he did in middle school, and he had his own way to deal with them now. I was okay with his answer, even relieved. He apparently knew how to pick himself up. I was good with that.

Looking back now, I was such a fool. My ignorant and uneducated opinion about mental health kept Matt from talking about his depression. I should never have accepted Matt's way of dealing with issues without digging deeper into exactly how he was doing it. Had I done just that, I may have found out then he was using drugs and alcohol to escape and self-medicate. I didn't find out until Matt's first time in rehab. Matt had everyone, including me, fooled. He hid his dependency very well. How I handled this could have changed everything.

My second biggest regret or missed opportunity was about three months before Matt's car accident. Matt showed up for work completely wasted. Matt always hid his dependency very well, so to see him like that was out of character for him. Matt confessed he had a cocaine problem. He said had used up all his savings to support his habit. Matt assured us he was done with drugs. I suggested that he go into rehab. Neither Tim nor Matt wanted anything to do with rehab. If Matt went into treatment, he would probably lose his job. That would also look bad on Tim who was Matt's foreman. I secretly was glad the rehab solution was vetoed. Back then, I truly believed if a person wanted to stop using drugs or alcohol, they just stopped. Matt said he was done, so he was just that done. Back then, I didn't understand addiction and how it affected the brain. Most addicts must work hard every day to get and remain sober. Had Matt gone into treatment that day, he probably wouldn't have been in the car accident three months later. The injuries in the car accident lead to overprescribed opiates and later to a heroin addiction.

My third biggest regret was when I tried to do an intervention with Ryan. He turned things around and called the police on me for kidnapping his son. The police gave me an opportunity to force Ryan into rehab. I walked away from that opportunity because

I didn't want a legal battle with Ryan. Tim, Ryan, and a few others were upset with me for trying to do an unwanted intervention that really bothered me. Ryan stopped speaking to me for a couple of weeks, which hurt. The hurt I felt for Ryan not speaking to me for a couple of weeks doesn't compare to the hurt I now feel not being able to speak to him for the rest of my life. Saving Ryan could have possibly saved Matt too. Matt's addiction carried a lot more baggage than Ryan's. The guilt over Ryan's passing was probably Matt's greatest mental health issue. My decision to walk away from helping Ryan may have cost both their lives.

Moving Forward

I continue to work toward ending this awful epidemic. I work closely with my friend Ann Youngblood. We are constantly fundraising to financially assist those still suffering. I try to participate and speak at as many events as I am asked, which have included schools, churches, rallies, treatment centers, podcast, TV, and radio, (podcast: "Drug Stories My Twins Sons").

One school I work particularly close with is Northeast Senior High (the same high school my kids attended). They have an amazing signature program headed by Brandi Dorsey. The program has done so much to bring awareness and education to the community.

I still have my own thoughts on what needs to change in order to end this epidemic. I stand by my belief that a parent or loved one has the right to make decisions for someone is abusing drugs or suffering from mental health issues. If a person is not of sound mind, then the court should allow their next of kin to act as an abdicate to speak for and make decisions for them. I know it's believed that a person can only get clean if they want to. My sons have been forced into treatment by the legal system. It was against their will. After receiving treatment and they were feeling better, they were grateful for the help. The legal system shouldn't be the only one who can force them into treatment. I truly believe my sons would still be alive today if I was able to act on their behalf.

The most informative things I've learned about addiction is it's not a moral failure. It's a brain disease. It's linked to mental health issues. It can be passed on from one generation to another through genetics. These significant facts will eventually help with proper treatment and could reduce relapsing.

I do believe these are a few of the reasons my sons easily became addicts. If there is some advice I could give to parents of children in elementary school, it would be to take time to educate yourself on mental health and addiction. Research your family tree. If there are *any* family members who suffers from either one, then your children could be at risk. Talk to your children. More important, listen to your children. We all want the best for them, and sometimes we push them to do it all. It can be overwhelming trying to balance school, sports, clubs and social activities, etc. Listen to them if they say it's too much. If they have a tendency of getting too anxious over little things or if they show signs of being depressed, pay attention, talk to them and react. Be the parent who prevents addiction. Be the parent who understands mental health and is willing to step up. I wish I had been.

One statement that is often said to Katie and I is, "I don't know how you do it." Well, we weren't given a choice. We could either curl up and wilt away, or we can find our new normal while keeping Ryan and Matt's memory in our hearts. We know that with this huge hole in our hearts, we'll never be truly happy ever again. Every day we are reminded of who's missing, who's not coming back. We will have to settle on what's left while making the most of it. There are four little boys counting on us to do just that. Ryan and Matt would want that for us.

Regardless on if you believe addiction is a moral failure or a disease, the number of lives lost and affected by the epidemic is heartbreaking. At the time of this writing, on average, 192 people die a day from an overdose. More lives were lost to this epidemic in 2015 than the loss in the Vietnam War. I read somewhere that on the average, five kids in every elementary school class will have lost a parent or sibling to an overdose. More children today are being raised by grandparents and family member who are not their parents than ever before in history. Why is any of this acceptable?

I am sickened by the pharmaceutical companies that profited while our loved died of overdoses. They lied to us about how addictive opioid are just to pay their own bank accounts. Meanwhile, families like mine lost everything to try to save their loved ones. We cleaned out our bank accounts to pay for treatment, lawyers, pawnshops, and finally, funeral homes. We will probably never be compensated in any way for our loss with any of the current lawsuits against them. Not that a monetary settlement will take away our pain.

A person should never be shamed into remaining silent if they suffer from depression or mental health issues. They should not have to claim they are suicidal just to get help for depression. They should be able to express that they are depressed and be treated accordingly. We don't make a person with high blood pressure wait until they have a heart attack until we treat them, nor do shame a person with high blood pressure into remaining silent and sucking it up. We encourage preventative or early treatment that is always more effective. This could also lower the number of people who turn to self-medicating with drugs and alcohol.

It's been proven we can't jail our way out of this problem.

Ryan and Matt, not a day goes by that I don't cry for the two you. The two of you (and Katie) gave me the greatest love, pleasure, and happiness any mother could ask for. Ryan, I will forever miss your charismatic ways, your handsome, good looks, your funny personality, and your caring and kind ways. Matt, I will forever miss your gentle, caring, and kind ways, your ability to listen to others, your handsome, good looks, and your compassion for others. I love you both to the moon and back. Until we meet again.

2010–2020
THE DECADE WE LOST HALF
A MILLION AMERICANS TO
THE OPIOID CRISIS

About the Author

D enise Williams was born and raised in Baltimore, Maryland. For the past thirty-eight years, she has lived in Pasadena, Maryland. A mother of three children and grandmother to four. Denise has worked as a floral designer for the past twenty-eight years. After her family suffered from the devastating effects of addiction, Denise now dedicates her time to bring awareness and education to other families suffering from addiction.

CPSIA information can be obtained
at www.ICGtesting.com
Printed in the USA
LVHW020910210920
666634LV00002B/187